STABILITY AND CHANGE IN CONGRESS

STABILITY AND CHANGE IN CONGRESS

Barbara Hinckley

CORNELL UNIVERSITY

HARPER & ROW, PUBLISHERS

New York, Evanston, San Francisco, London

Standard Book Number: 06-042835-X
Library of Congress Catalog Card Number: 70–68360

CONTENTS

AUTHOR'S NOTE

*C*ongress has enjoyed considerable attention from political scientists in recent years. Its committees, subcommittees, and norms, its roll call behavior and history, its leadership and legislation—all have been subjected to increasingly skillful and specialized analysis. The number of studies is increasing at some geometric rate. But this rush of research has not been brought together into any synthetic ordering. Books "on Congress" are, for the most part, collections of separate studies.

The time may have come to try. This book attempts a preliminary synthesis. It should give the beginning student a more satisfactory accounting of Congress than anthologies can supply and should offer the advanced student a clearer sense of the state of congressional research—of where things are going and where they might be going.

My thanks to John Manley and Robert Peabody for a thorough reading of the manuscript and some excellent criticism, and to Dorothea Autilio, Production Editor at Harper & Row, whose skill and pleasantness smoothed the process of publication. My thanks also to those students at Massachusetts and Cornell whose insights and questions enriched the course and the book that grew from it. But perhaps the largest debt in a book of this kind is owed to the literature on which it is based. In this sense, then, responsibility for the strengths and shortcomings of the present work will have to be shared between us.

B.H.

CHAPTER 1

INTRODUCTION

*C*ongress has been in the business of national government for two centuries—spanning in full the nation's life, its growth and trials, and expanding responsibilities. And yet, through all the changes, Congress has shown a marked persistence. The ninety-second Congress, as its name implies, can boast a long ancestral line. It still observes the eighteenth-century notion of a representative assembly and the nineteenth-century innovation of popular democracy. But beyond this basic persistence, the twentieth-century Congress has exhibited a stability in even sharper and more specific form. Its leadership remains decentralized after the one House experiment with more centralized forms under the Speaker at the turn of the century. The seniority system, despite the recurring attacks against it, continues to name the chairmen of the standing committees. The two parties continue to organize the Congress, supply lists for committee assignments, and offer the cues that best explain congressmen's decisions on roll call votes. Chairmen are still accused of being petty "barons," as they were in Woodrow Wilson's day, withholding bounty from the presidential overlord. And even some of the members have remained the same. With Franklin Roosevelt in the White House and a New Deal and new Supreme Court in the making, Congress became the last refuge for conservatives in the national government. With Richard Nixon in the White House and another Court in the making, it now may be in the process of becoming the last refuge for liberals. The players may shift but the refuge remains the same.

All this is not to say that no changes have occurred. The Legislative Reorganization Act of 1947 drastically cut the number of standing committees and in the process disposed of some members' committee chairmanships. In the Senate, floor leaders have developed key roles. Recent congresses have somewhat relaxed the rule of silence once imposed on freshman members and have sought ways to make chairmen more responsive to their committees. Members must now record their position on teller votes. And in matters of policy, congressmen have initiated important new legislation, such as in the area of air-and-water-pollution control, and a chairman of the Senate Foreign Relations Committee undertook hearings on a President's handling of the Vietnam War. But what this review does is call attention to the phenomenon of stability in change or to the "dynamic" of congressional persistence. For stability over time implies processes of reinforcement which may be every bit as dynamic and powerful as processes of change. And the degree of stability evidenced by the United States Congress poses a phenomenon richly deserving attention and explanation. If in the 1970s a Henry Clay would not be elected Speaker on his first day in the House, he still would recognize certain features of the place. And a Henry Cabot Lodge or an Arthur Vandenberg could, with minor adaptations, continue where they had left off some sixty and thirty years before.

CONGRESS AND "REFORM"

In reaction to all this stability, the plea for change, or "Reform," has been the dominant theme in twentieth-century writing on Congress. It is the motif almost ritually aired by students of politics and journalists alike. Public affairs magazines give it at least one thorough annual venting. Typically it is argued that for a number of reasons and in a number of ways, Congress is ill-suited to assume major responsibilities in a vast and changing nation. Further, not only does it fail to help, but indeed it hurts by obstructing the executive branch which is so equipped. And finally, even that negative, obstructive impact cannot be said to represent the legislative will of a majority of Americans, because Congress is so constructed that established minorities control procedure and policy-making. Book titles on the subject strike a singular note of gloom: *The Sapless Branch, House out of Order, The Deadlock of Democracy, Congress in Crisis.*[1]

The critical commentary, as David Truman points out, springs from three distinct sets of circumstances.[2] First, dissatisfaction is in part attributable to the "parliamentary crisis" afflicting all twentieth-century democratic legislatures. The complexity and interdependence of contemporary society require expertise and coordinated decision-making that legislatures cannot provide. The nationalization of socioeconomic problems sharpens the need for coordination and a nationwide view. Foreign policy salience and the need for complex national security decisions have increased executive dominance. And the full commitment of national resources in war has blurred the line between "foreign" and "domestic" policy and further augmented executive authority. The urgency of events in the nuclear age may make "deliberation" and deliberative assemblies seem a luxury a nation can no longer afford. More generally, the mood and tempo of politics have shifted—from deliberation to decision-making, from debate among elder statesmen to action by energetic task forces, from the amateur generalist to the specialized expert. In other words the mood, or the initiative, has shifted from legislative to executive.

Second, dissatisfaction springs from the particular American constitutional arrangement of the separation of powers. The President and the Congress are separate institutions, which share powers under a system that essentially permits one to serve as a veto, or check, on the other. These separate institutions have constitutionally staggered elections and separate constituencies. Whereas in the aggregate, Congress, like the President, represents the nation as a whole, each senator or representative represents one state or one

[1] See Roger H. Davidson, David M. Kovenock, and Michael K. O'Leary, *Congress in Crisis: Politics and Congressional Reform* (Belmont, Calif.: Wadsworth, 1966), for an excellent analysis and commentary on the reform literature.

[2] David B. Truman (ed.), *The Congress and America's Future* (Englewood Cliffs, N.J.: Prentice-Hall, 1965), pp. 1–4.

district. Hence there is a basic ambivalence built into the congressman's role. He represents a state or district in a national assembly. Conflict between "national" and "local" views has in one way been aggravated by the expansion of the national government's activities. As increasing numbers of local interests are affected by or become dependent upon national policy, new local pressures on the national government are generated. Defense contracts and installations are vital to the economy of many localities and even entire states. Federal subsidies support whole sectors of industry and commerce. And federal grants-in-aid finance major undertakings of state governments.

This separate basis for congressional power explains the historic rivalry between the two institutions. It explains why Congress is the most powerful of all national legislatures. But, in an executive-dominant age, it also explains aggravation with an institution capable of obstructing the executive. And it explains the charge of "provincialism" or "localism" leveled at Congress, which, to put it quite simply, was built that way.

Third, dissatisfaction derives from specific congressional structures and procedures: for example, the obstructive power of committee chairmen, the seniority system, the Rules Committee in the House, and the Senate filibuster. As Truman points out, this area has drawn most of the critical fire.[3] In the critics' view, these practices further fragmentize the power to govern and give strategically situated minorities a disproportionately large influence. "Subgovernments" in such areas as sugar or defense can be maintained through long-standing collaboration between chairmen, agency personnel, and private interest groups.[4] From his chairmanship of the Foreign Aid Subcommittee of the House Appropriations Committee, Otto Passman could affect American foreign policy by the perennial slashing of Presidential aid budgets.

Within this third category there is a substrand of criticism from

[3] *Ibid.*, p. 3.
[4] Douglass Cater, *Power in Washington* (New York: Random House, 1964), pp. 17–20, 26–48.

those who urge a streamlining and modernization of congressional procedure. The "modernizers," mainly a number of congressmen and political scientists, seek expanded congressional staff, improved information-gathering facilities, and automatic data processing of budgetary information.[5] But unlike the traditional reformers, the modernizers have no basic quarrel with Congress's representative character and do not implicitly favor stronger Presidential government. Indeed, they wish to strengthen Congress as a governing agent independent of the President by increasing its information and improving its capacity for oversight.

While the main thrust of reformist criticism is understandable, it leads away from rather than toward increased understanding of the subject. First, it assumes knowledge of Congress which, I would argue, should be updated by the past ten to fifteen years work in that area. Second, it oversimplifies at the risk of considerable distortion. For example, the reformists' schema of "centrifugal" and "centripetal" forces which, much as the forces of good and evil, battle it out in committee or on the floor (party leaders representing the centripetal and good; chairmen, the seniority system, and the Rules Committee, the centrifugal and evil) overlooks both the accommodation that takes place between party leaders and chairmen and the fact that committees vary considerably in control exercised by chairmen and in the kinds of majorities or minorities they try to represent. Obsession with congressional obstructionism perhaps blinds such critics to the fact that it is not uncommon for majorities to be built, compromises to be made, Presidential programs to be passed. Thus they do not ask under what conditions such events can or cannot occur.

Finally, reformist criticism tends to be time-bound—too constrained in its attention to the immediate experience of Democratic

---

[5] See Davidson *et al., op. cit.,* pp. 15–37, for discussion; and see Joint Committee on the Organization of Congress, Eighty-ninth Congress, First Session, *Second Interim Report,* Senate Report 948 (1965), pp. 7, 8; Joint Committee on the Organization of Congress, Eighty-ninth Congress, Second Session, *Final Report,* Senate Report 1414 (1966).

control of Congress and the White House. Proponents of reform, who incidentally are apt to be liberals, look to a Democratic Presidency for support of their political views and attack the congressional obstructionism and conservatism that prevents Presidential policies from being enacted into law. The two "practices"—obstructionism and conservatism—are assumed to go together. Thus the seniority system is a favorite target because it allows committee chairmen to be independent of Presidential and party control. Secure in their position, conservative Southern Democratic chairmen can delay or defeat liberal legislation at the committee stage without fear of reprisal. Thus, a Howard W. Smith, Democratic Chairman of the Rules Committee, could be home in Virginia "inspecting a burned barn" when civil rights legislation was due for a committee hearing. But with a conservative Republican President and a Democratic ninety-first and ninety-second Congress, we have begun to hear cries against the seniority system from the conservative side of the aisle. President Nixon's anticrime bill, feared by liberals as a threat to civil liberties, was enmired for some time in the House Judiciary Committee, whose liberal chairman, Emanuel Celler, is from Brooklyn. The bill ultimately reached the floor, but this case suggests a new situation: perhaps liberals will look to the seniority system for protection against Presidential "innovation," and conservative voices will more frequently be raised for reform. The seniority system always has buttressed congressional independence; its virtues may now become more visible to the liberal eye.

All this is not to say that the reform view has no merit. Certainly, that view has probed important congressional questions. But, as noted previously, statements urging "reform of Congress" would be more convincing if they were better grounded in knowledge of the institution they wish to reform. At minimum, the reformer should know the kinds of change that are possible and the conditions under which change can occur. He should seek first to understand the dynamic of congressional stability—that is, to determine what makes patterns of action persist over time and beyond the time of individual actors. For the processes of reinforcement and adaptation may suggest key points to look for change.

INSTITUTIONAL CONTEXT

Such stability, of course, is not peculiar to the institution of the United States Congress. Institutions, by definition, exist over time. They are human creations, existing through stable patterns of interaction among individuals and groups. Actions are defined, refined, and supported with the passage of time. They become regularized, routinized, stabilized. Expectations about who does what and who should do what are formed and influence subsequent actions, and so on. Thus, one conversation between Speaker Sam Rayburn and Rules Committee Chairman Howard Smith may mean little. But regular consultation between the two contributes to a decentralized leadership through which key decisions are made and becomes a fact congressmen have to take into consideration in subsequent interactions. Committee choices shape an informal "prestige ranking" of committees, which influences subsequent choices. A highly valued committee assignment may be won by the most influential congressman. But the fact that it is highly valued and the fact that influential congressmen are members increase the committee's attractiveness in later assignments. Such patterns of action reinforce each other over time.

Emphasis on action should not lead one to overlook the "thingness" of institutions. Institutions have a distinctive identity, which makes them more than the sum of their parts. Congress exists not only as multidimensional patterns of action. It exists concretely and integrally as a "thing"—a governing body, a representative legislature. It is a structure on Capitol Hill. It is a "real" object to Presidents, agency administrators, and interest groups, which must contend with it—and to the congressmen who give it loyalty and support.

In a number of ways institutions are analogous to human beings. Human beings similarly may be defined by multidimensional patterns of action. They similarly exist in a time dimension and possess a knack of endurance, and similarly have a concrete integrity and a distinctive character, which is more than the sum of the parts. Philip Selznick's description of institutions may be helpful. He speaks of the "responsive interaction of persons and groups" and continues:

> In the course of time, this responsive interaction is patterned. A social structure is created. This patterning is *historical* in that it reflects the specific experiences of the particular organization; it is *functional* in that it aids the organization to adapt itself to its internal and external social environment; and it is *dynamic,* in that it generates new and active forces.[6]

The institution's life, as the individual's, has a past and a future and a set of processes whereby that life is maintained. The process permits stability or change. The similarity is striking and readily understandable. Institutions share some characteristics of their human creators and sustainers, whose own interests are served by continuing or changing certain interactions, practices, and results.

A search for the dynamic of congressional stability can begin with an examination of characteristics that define the institution. Congress is an (1) elective, (2) geographically representative, (3) bicameral, (4) legislative assembly, which (5) shares power with the executive in national government. These characteristics are curious in combination. There is power there, but it is fragmented —first by bicameralism, then by geography, and finally by its electoral basis into 435 plus 100, or 535 separate components. "Power" is construed simply to mean the ability to influence people or events in ways specified by the agent. Congress is a *collegial* institution. It is essentially an assembly of equals. Each senator and representative has his own constituency and his own claim to legislative legitimacy equal to that of any other member. This collegial character poses constraints on the organization of influence in the Congress, for who leads an assembly where all are constitutionally equal? With the egalitarian solution that major decisions will be taken by majority vote, the number and distribution of members aligned one way or the other becomes critically important for policy outcomes.

The elective character of Congress means further that leaders

---

[6] Philip Selznick, *Leadership in Administration* (New York: Harper & Row, 1957), pp. 38–40. Selznick's study focuses on institutions and the dynamic of institutional changes.

neither control the selection of members nor possess the power to guarantee or withhold tenure. There is no guarantee of secure membership in the organization as a reward for long or distinguished service. A representative of 20 years' standing still must return to the voters every second year to ask to remain a member of the House. Congressional membership is determined instead by the party system in its state and local operation and, ultimately, by the American voters. Without the power to hire or fire, leaders have only limited rewards and sanctions to apply. Consider membership in the congressional party. If the voters of Virginia's Third Congressional District elect Congressman X as a Democrat to represent them, X can go to the House and act as the most stalwart of Republicans if he chooses and there is little that the House Democratic leadership can do.

This elective character also means that stability, turnover, and the chance for new blood and a change of view are decided not by the leadership but by forces outside the institution itself. Technically, the entire membership of the House could be overturned every two years. This was part of the framer's "dangerous" experiment with popular rule. The danger, as it was perceived at the time (and it was part of the argument for a Senate), was that the House would be too swayed by the changeable winds of public passion to permit sober perspective to develop with time. It is ironic that the House, feared in the eighteenth century as the changeable, unstable chamber, should be criticized in the twentieth for its unresponsiveness and resistance to change. Throughout the past several decades the large majority of representatives have *not* been overturned every second year.

The above discussion suggests that in Congress the individual member will be more important, the "leader" less important than in some institutions. Decentralized structures of influence will be necessary to maintain the institution's distinctive character. The composition and distribution of the membership will have a direct effect on policy and will determine to a large extent who the leaders will be.

And yet since all this fragmented power must be structured in some way if the institution is to maintain itself as a governing agent, Congress needs a division of labor and leadership. It needs a system for mobilizing individual congressmen into majorities, and a set of norms prescribing valued institutional behavior. With the membership selected according to "outside" criteria, it can be expected that compensatory influences will develop from within. The senators from Mississippi, Michigan, and Massachusetts need to work together in the same party or in the same committee despite widely different backgrounds, interests, and constituency claims. Congressional norms influence a diverse membership to support the same practices and values. From a widely heterogeneous membership those who possess attributes most useful to the institution are selected as leaders. A seniority system guarantees that influence goes to those who both have been there longest and are likely to be most similar to each other and most supportive of the institution. And these structures, in turn, will redistribute the underlying distribution of members. They are shaped in part by the membership according to institutional needs, but once in existence they exercise an independent impact—both on the membership and on resulting legislation. Leadership and the division of labor by committees distribute influence unevenly. Norms affect members' subsequent actions. The seniority system, by determining the selection of committee chairmen, initiates additional forces of its own.

A study of Congress, then, might well begin with the membership and then look to the key institutional structures by which the underlying distribution of members is redistributed along seniority, committee, and party lines. Whatever interrelations can be discovered here—as they work over time to adapt, influence, support, or reinforce—may supply the key linkage points necessary for explaining congressional stability and change.

This study concentrates on the contemporary (post-1946) Congress, although historical perspective is supplied where necessary. Spanning five different President's administrations and a quarter of a century, it should provide a sufficiently long and varied time period for analysis. It is this contemporary Congress that appears to one group of observers a historical anomaly, to another, an institution that cries for reform, to a third (including Presidents), an immensely powerful governing agent, to a fourth, sluggish, impossible to move, a source of great frustrations, and to still another the only elective democratic institution capable of criticizing or checking the executive. This is the subject of the book.

CHAPTER 2

CONGRESSIONAL ELECTIONS

Analysis of the membership of any organization should focus first on how it is selected. Who selects the members? By what criteria? Subject to what reconsideration? The process of selection is a process of definition. It systematically chooses some and screens out others and consequently builds in patterns of action which affect the organization's life. Certainly it is crucial to the stability of an organization—that is, its ability to maintain its goals and characteristic patterns of action over time.

Mode of selection is particularly critical for representative assemblies because their legitimacy is based on the fact that it is the people who make the selection. The membership of the U.S. Congress is selected from outside the organization itself. No leaders or personnel committees determine the size or makeup of the next crop of freshman congressmen. True, the leadership and congressional campaign committees may influence candidate selection and the funding of campaigns, but these factors count at most as marginal influences on individual elections.

Further, the relationship between the congressman and his constituency is shaped by the method of selection. Hence the concern with such questions as what criteria do the American voters use in their selection of congressmen? How important are the campaign, the candidate's stands on issues, or a congressman's record in office?

And finally, because Congress is not only a continuing and representative organization but also one that shares power with another governing agent, the President, the selection process affects Presidential-congressional relations. One of the strongest bonds between the two separated powers, common party identification and the partisan composition of its membership, is one of the major determinants of Congress's willingness and capacity to cooperate with the President.

Accordingly, this chapter focuses on elections as they shape certain key characteristics of the congressional membership—characteristics that in turn affect the organization's policy.

One introductory caution is in order for the reader who has gained most of his impressions of the subject from political journalism. In its emphasis on the unique and the newsworthy, political journalism directs attention to close races, primary fights, election upsets, phenomena that enrich the lore of politics and are important to understand in their own right. But they are in a sense the political "festivals" —breaks in the normal routine. On most days there are no festivals. And in most races there are no primary fights or election tossups. To appreciate the significance of elections, it is necessary to study the kind of election most congressmen have faced and may look forward to facing again, not only the exceptions.

THE VOTERS

Preliminary insight can be gained from an examination of those who set the criteria for selection, the voters. The American voter has been subjected to intensive study for almost a quarter of a century. This research has underscored the importance of party identification. Approximately 75 percent of nationwide samples polled are willing to call themselves Democrats or Republicans. And a large majority of these vote their party: Democrats for Democratic candidates, Republicans for Republicans. This partisanship is largely nonprogrammatic in nature. Party loyalty, typically learned early from the family, is relatively free of ideological or issue content.[1] Note the two-way reach of party loyalty in elections. It serves as a

[1] Donald Stokes and Warren Miller, "Party Government and the Saliency of Congress," in Angus Campbell et al. (eds.), Elections and the Political Order (New York: John Wiley, 1967), p. 198.

cue not only to voting for a number of offices– local, state, federal–
in one election, but also to voting for a sequence of elections for one
office. Thus we speak of "Republican states" or "Democratic districts" and apply knowledge of the constituency's partisan composition to explain past or predict future elections. Furthermore, voting
turnout correlates strongly and positively with party loyalty, level
of education, and interest in politics. College graduates are more
likely to vote than high-school graduates, high-school graduates
more than grade-school graduates; strong Republicans and Democrats than weak Republicans and Democrats, and weak partisans
more than independents. The comparatively lower turnout of independents serves to augment the weight of party identifiers in elections.[2]

What of those, often college-educated and usually independents,
whose interest in public affairs has led to disillusionment with party
politics? The answer is simply that such a group, no matter how
large and obvious they may seem to some, is so small compared to
other political types in the American adult population as not to be
observable in nationwide statistics.

Voter turnout data indicate a markedly low level of voter interest
in and information about congressional affairs. Approximately 60 to
70 percent of the electorate vote in Presidential elections. Most also
vote for senator and representative at the same time. But in off-year
congressional elections (elections held in those even-numbered
years when there is no Presidential race) voter turnout drops sharply,
averaging slightly under or barely 50 percent. This pattern of two-
year upswings and declines in turnout has held throughout the
twentieth century and through the 1960s.[3]

Survey results also point up widespread disinterest in congressional affairs. A majority of respondents do not know which party
controls Congress and cannot name their senators and representatives. And only approximately one-half of those who vote in congres-

[2] Angus Campbell et al., The American Voter (New York: John Wiley, 1960),
pp. 89–115.

[3] V. O. Key, Jr., Parties, Politics and Pressure Groups. (5th ed., New York:
Thomas Y. Crowell, 1964), p. 568.

sional election have "read or heard something" about either candidate. The incumbent is by far the better known. Approximately one-fourth have "read or heard something" about *both* candidates. And what was read or heard is noteworthy. Less than 10 percent are able to explain their vote in terms of any discernible issue.[4] Impressions are expressed mainly in such terms as so-and-so is "a good man," "is experienced," "has done a good job." Equally important is the fact that the congressmen know that this situation exists. As one House member remarked in a discussion of the importance of issues in a campaign, "every once in a while you get shocked by the lack of information people have about political events and candidates, and you realize this is not the way they make up their minds." Another pointed out that even those constituents sufficiently interested to write to their representative are sometimes mistaken about his name.[5]

Of course, some congressional races are marked by high visibility of candidates and/or clearly perceived issues. An extreme case involved the write-in candidacy of Dale Alford against Arkansas Representative Brooks Hayes in 1958. Hayes had helped as intermediary between the White House and Governor Faubus in the Little Rock integration crisis. A sample from Hayes' constituency was asked if they had "read or heard something" about either candidate: both Hayes and Alford got 100 percent scores. Further, the survey made clear that Hayes was regarded as "more moderate" on civil rights, that this perception was held by both supporters and opponents, and that it brought about his defeat.[6] The contrast with the nationwide recognition scores reported above is dramatic but apparently still an exception to the normal pattern.

For most voters most of the time the saliency of congressional candidates and issues is low. If only half are aware of something about one candidate, and only one-fourth of something about both

[4] Stokes and Miller, *op. cit.*, pp. 199, 204, 205.

[5] Charles L. Clapp, *The Congressman: His Work as He Sees It* (New York: Doubleday, 1963), p. 420.

[6] Miller and Stokes, "Constituency Influence in Congress," in *Elections and the Political Order*, pp. 369, 370.

candidates, how do the others decide how to vote? What factors influence the voting decision in the absence of specific information about candidates and issues?

MAJOR INFLUENCES ON CONGRESSIONAL ELECTIONS

CONSTITUTIONAL STAGGERING OF ELECTIONS

One major influence is the constitutional staggering of elections for the Senate and House. The President's term is four years, a representative's two years, and a senator's six years. Senate elections are staggered so that one-third faces an election every second year. This arrangement has considerable ramifications for the composition of the House and Senate, as will be made clear shortly. The Democratic "Class of 1958" is frequently mentioned as one of the most fortunate Senate groups, electorally speaking. Democratic senators first elected in 1958 on a surge of Democratic sentiment (or anti-Republican sentiment) were able to sit out the lean years of 1960 and 1962 and try for reelection in the year of the Johnson landslide. Notice by contrast the rigor of a Democratic senator's struggle if his first election placed him in the 1956 sequence. If he survived the Eisenhower landslide, he ran again in 1962, with no assistance from a Democratic Presidential candidate, and then had to weather the antiadministration climate of 1968.

PARTY LOYALTY

Staggering of elections also gives an alternating weight to two other major influences: party loyalty and the Presidential vote. Party loyalty is important in Presidential and off-year elections. Congressional elections follow the broader pattern exhibited in state and nationwide contests. The voter's party identification serves as a major cue for voting choice. Often it may be his only cue, because the candidate's party is the one fact other than his name that ballots supply. What this means is that state by state, county by county, district by district, more Democratic or more Republican electorates tend to vote more strongly Democratic or Republican for a number of different offices and across a number of elections. For example, states ranked high in Democratic party identifiers will tend to rank high in Democratic vote for President and senator. Even in strongly Republican years such as 1956, although the total Democratic vote may drop sharply, these states will still be more Democratic in voting than others. Party loyalty is particularly important in the off year. Those less politically interested and less partisan, deprived of the stimulus of a Presidential election campaign, are more likely not to vote. The result is strong and clear partisan voting from the "hard-core" off-year electorate.[7]

Some observers have noted a rise in split-ticket voting in the past fifteen years. Surveys also suggest an 8 to 10 percent rise in independent identifiers (and drop in Democratic identifiers) between 1964 and 1968.[8] This may well reflect a short-term dissatisfaction with the Democratic party, especially with its conduct of the Vietnam War, handling of the law-and-order issue, and the 1968 Chicago nominating convention. Or it may signal a longer-term weakening of partisan loyalties. Despite short-term shifts, party loyalties have demonstrated considerable stability. Between 1948 and 1968, percentages of those calling themselves Democrats, Republicans, and independents varied only within a 10-point range.[9] Whatever realignment or movement away from party loyalty the future may bring, congressional elections from 1947 to the present and well into the 1970s still need to be viewed in terms of the strong and persisting party loyalty of American voters.

PRESIDENTIAL "COATTAILS"

Generations of political observers have noted the "pulling power" of the Presidential vote. As the vote for one party's Presidential candidate increases state by state or district by district, the vote for that party's Senate and/or House candidates also increases. Or,

---

[7] Angus Campbell, "Surge and Decline: A Study of Electoral Change," in Elections and the Political Order, pp. 40–62.

[8] Everett Ladd et al., "The American Party Coalitions: Social Change and Partisan Alignments," 1935–1970, American Political Science Association paper, September 1970, pp. 14–15.

[9] Ibid.

expressed another way, the greater the vote for a party's Presidential candidate, the less likely is defeat for its congressional candidates. If elections are viewed over a number of years, the close articulation between Presidential and congressional voting becomes vividly apparent. Upswings and declines in the Presidential popular vote are closely reflected in the congressional vote.

But how does one know that this close correspondence is not simply the result of party loyalty? While party loyalty helps explain the phenomenon, there exists a separate, observable influence of Presidential coattails. Party loyalty can be controlled by measuring the deviation in Presidential and congressional voting from what may be called a "base party vote": the estimated percentage of voters in the state identifying with a party. Thus, if it is estimated that 44 percent of Montana's voting population are Democratic identifiers, and the state votes 60 percent Democratic for President and 56 percent Democratic for Senator, its deviation in Democratic vote for President is +16.0 and for Senator, +12.0. By looking at the deviations, one has, in effect, kept party loyalty out of the picture. As Table 2.1 shows, by correlating deviations in Presidential and senatorial voting, as the strength of the Democratic Presidential

TABLE 2.1   Relationship between Presidential and Senate Voting Measured by Deviations from the Democratic Base Party Vote, 1956–1966

PRESIDENTIAL VOTE DEVIATION (IN PERCENTAGE POINTS)	NUMBER OF CONTESTS	SENATE VOTE: MEAN DEVIATION FROM BASE PARTY VOTE
Extremely Strong Democratic ($\geq +15.0$)	14	+16.0
Strong Democratic (+14.9 to +10.0)	8	+12.4
Moderate (+9.9 to +5.0)	7	+5.1
Moderate (+4.9 to 0)	16	+6.0
Strong Republican (−.1 to −4.9)	13	+3.2
Extremely Strong Republican (≤ -5.0)	12	−2.6

SOURCE: Barbara Hinckley, "Incumbency and the Presidential Vote in Senate Elections: "Defining Parameters of Subpresidential Voting," *American Political Science Review* (September 1970): p. 841.

candidate increases, the strength of the Democratic senatorial candidate also increases.[10]

Of course, a Presidential coattail is an elusive thing, which is not "proved" by analysis such as that just described. And in some elections there may even be a *congressional* coattail—for example, strong voting for a popular Senate incumbent may help the party's Presidential candidate. State and district surveys would be needed to confirm the possibility. All that can be said at this point is that the persistence of the pattern nationwide and the greater salience of Presidential contests have led most analysts to agree that the coattail effect is predominantly from the Presidential side.

Considered together, party loyalty and the Presidential vote help explain one of the most curious patterns in American elections—that is, the off-year (midterm) loss of House seats by the President's party in every midterm election since the Civil War, with the exception of 1934. The very persistence of the pattern casts doubt on the fairly widespread notion that the midterm election can be interpreted as an electoral "verdict" on the President's administration at the halfway point. Thus construed, the midterm verdict is always withdrawal of support. The net number of seats lost has varied widely—from 75 in 1922 to 4 in 1962—and perhaps offers some clue to popular support, if one knew how to interpret it. How, for example, would one interpret the 1966 results? The Republicans pointed to the Democrats' 47-seat net loss as a Republican "victory," but the Democratic countered that their loss was so much smaller than might be expected that the election demonstrated continuing confidence in the Johnson administration.

Any nonpartisan interpretation of House midterm elections must first consider the fact that two very different electorates go to the polls in a Presidential year and in an off year. A midterm election brings the habitual, partisan voter to the polls, whereas the Presidential election attracts both habitual and marginal voters. As

[10] For a more detailed explanation of the analysis, see Barbara Hinckley, "Incumbency and the Presidential Vote in Senate Elections: Defining Parameters of Subpresidential Voting," *American Political Science Review*, (September 1970): 836–842.

Angus Campbell argues, in any Presidential election one or the other candidate has an advantage of party, personality, or salient issue, which attracts the less politically interested voters, as well as some habitual voters, who then support him and his party's ticket. But in the off year that small proportion of habitual voters who defected return to the party fold, but, more important, the less interested portion of the electorate stays at home. Both events hurt the party whose Presidential and House candidates had the advantage in the previous national election.[11]

Seen in this light, much of the Presidential party's loss at midterm may be a built-in loss "dictated" by the victory two years before. The more House candidates carried to victory on Presidential coattails, the more House seats that may be lost in the midterm election when the coattails are absent. In other words, the degree of midterm loss may be directly related to the degree of Presidential popularity (that is, his coattail "pulling power") in the preceding election.

Such a midterm built-in loss or "countertendency" is indicated by the election results of the past several decades. As Table 2.2 shows, the largest net midterm losses tend to follow large Presidential victories, and so on down the line. And the smallest, the four-seat loss in 1962, followed a Democratic Presidential victory that was one of the narrowest in American political history. In most districts Kennedy lagged behind the Democratic House candidate— a reasonable indication that no Presidential coattails were assisting congressional Democrats into office. Thus in 1960 the Democrats did not gain any seats that could be lost in 1962. By contrast, the Johnson landslide of 1964 could be expected to build in a substantial loss for 1966. For an exception to the pattern, consider the 1946 loss of 55 seats, notably larger than might be expected from the 1944 Presidential vote, and sufficient to bring the Republicans to power in the House. Extreme postwar economic unrest, crippling strikes, and general dissatisfaction with status quo politics probably account

[11] Campbell, "Surge and Decline: A Study of Electoral Change Change," and "Voters and Elections: Past and Present," *Journal of Politics*, 26 (November 1964); 745–757. See also Barbara Hinckley, "Interpreting House Midterm Elections," *American Political Science Review* (September 1967): 694–700.

TABLE 2.2   Net Loss of Seats in the President's Party Related to the President's Percentage of Total Vote at the Preceding Election, 1920–1962

NET LOSS OF HOUSE SEATS FOR PRESIDENT'S PARTY	MIDTERM YEAR	PERCENT PRESIDENTIAL VOTE IN PRECEDING ELECTION
75	1922	60.4
71	1938	60.8
55	1946	53.5
49	1930	58.2
47	1958	57.4
45	1942	54.8
29	1950	49.5
18	1954	55.1
10	1926	54.0
4	1962	50.08

SOURCE: Barbara Hinckley, "Interpreting House Midtown Elections," *American Political Science Review* (September 1967).

for the results. In V. O. Key's words, the voters decided to "toss the rascals out"—the "rascals" being, then, the Democratic party. But whatever the results, the point to remember is that to interpret a midterm election in terms of partisan support, one must first discount the built-in loss "bequeathed" by the Presidential election.[12]

President Johnson and other adherents of stronger Presidential government have urged adoption of a constitutional amendment that would change the representative's term to four years, concurrent with the President's. The system of biennial elections results in the loss of partisan support in the House halfway through his term, and thus serves as a decisive check on the Presidency.

In sum, party loyalty and Presidential coattails combine to ensure at least common partisan ground for the Chief Executive and Congress through the first two years of his term. At midterm the loss of Presidential coattails enables more of the opposition party's candidates to gain Senate and House seats. But party loyalty still ensures some correspondence between the Presidency and congressional party strength. Figure 2.1 graphically shows the results: (1) stable House voting, hugging the 45 to 55 percent midpoint of the electoral spectrum; (2) more volatile Presidential voting with the

[12] Hinckley, "Interpreting House Midterm Elections," p. 700.

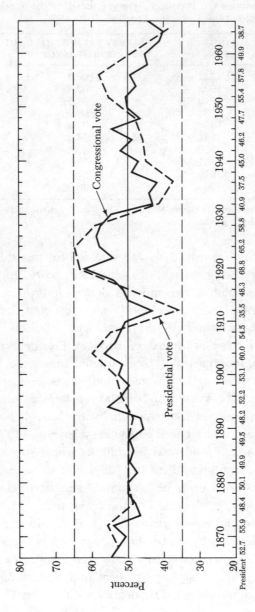

FIGURE 2.1 Republican Percentage of Major Party Vote for President and House Candidates Since the Civil War

SOURCE: Angus Campbell *et al.*, *Elections and the Political Order*, (New York: John Wiley, 1967), p. 183. The results for 1962 to 1966 were computed by the author.

Presidential vote climbing higher and descending lower in Republican and Democratic directions; but (3) a close correspondence between the two so that the party that wins the Presidency usually gains control of the House. In only seven of 35 Congresses in the 70-year span has there been divided party control. And because voters' party loyalties are stable over time, one party usually controls both the White House and Congress for a number of elections. Thus the political party is given, in V. O. Key's words, "a long-term chance to govern."

INCUMBENCY

A third factor is of major importance in congressional elections: the influence of incumbency. The senator or representative in office at election time has a major advantage over his nonincumbent opponent. Incumbents of each party enjoy 85 to 90 percent success rates in both Senate and House.[13] In other words, the incumbent will win 85 or 90 times out of 100. Not only is he more likely to win, but also his average performance at the polls is stronger than that of victorious nonincumbents.[14] Take the case of New Jersey's senatorial vote from 1956 to 1966. Keeping in mind that the basic party loyalties are assumed to be stable through the period, notice the wide differences in Democratic or Republican voting depending on incumbency:

Year	Percent Democratic Vote	Incumbency
1958	51.4	No incumbent
1960	43.2	Republican incumbent
1964	61.9	Democratic incumbent
1966	37.0	Republican incumbent

Such a similarity between Senate and House may surprise some who believe that the Senate, representing as it does whole states, not small homogeneous districts, is a much more electorally com-

---

[13] Lewis Froman, *The Congressional Process* (Boston: Little, Brown, 1967), p. 170. See also Charles Jones, *Every Second Year* (Washington, D.C.: Brookings Institution, 1967), p. 68.

[14] Hinckley, "Incumbency and the Presidential Vote in Senate Elections," p. 839.

petitive body. One explanation may be that the incidents of electoral mortality commonly cited to show the Senate's comparative competitiveness are drawn from a few large urban states with highly competitive, active parties. The incumbent success rate in New York, California, Pennsylvania, Illinois, Michigan, and Ohio —63 percent—is substantially lower than the overall rate. Incumbents still have a definite edge, but it is much narrower than in the other states.[15]

The voters' proclivity to reelect incumbents may conflict with the party and Presidential influences outlined above. It is incumbents who withstand the strong Presidential tide for the opposing party.[16] Much as the midterm election, then, incumbency provides a check on the carrying power of the Presidential vote. It also counters traditional party loyalties. Once in office a senator or representative tends to be reelected, despite the underlying partisan composition of his state or district. Traditionally Democratic Massachusetts, which accords most national Republican candidates a modest 30 to 40 percent of the vote, would troop to the polls to reelect Republican Senator Saltonstall by decisive margins. This pattern holds in many states and districts. The hurdle, of course, is the initial election. William Proxmire, a Democrat in then-Republican Wisconsin, was first elected in a 1957 special Senate election in which approximately one-third of the electorate turned out to vote. (Incidentally, the seat he was elected to by this fraction of the electorate had been vacated by the death of arch-conservative Republican Senator Joseph McCarthy.) Proxmire has been reelected three times —in 1958, 1964, and 1970. He was the beneficiary not only of the special circumstances that allowed a Democrat to be elected in the first place, but also of the good fortune of being in the Democratic Class of 1958.

A capsule summary of the three major influences on House races from 1924 through 1964 is provided by Table 2.3. Nonincumbent victories appear to be affected by each of the three influences. They

[15] *Ibid.,* p. 839.

[16] M. C. Cummings, *Congressmen and the Electorate,* (New York: Free Press, 1966), p. 58.

TABLE 2.3 Incumbency, Presidential Vote, and Previous Party Control: Their Effect on Nonincumbent House Victories, 1924 to 1964

	PERCENT NONINCUMBENT VICTORIES	
	PARTY THAT LOST PRESIDENCY	PARTY THAT WON PRESIDENCY
Opposing an Incumbent	4	20
Opposing a Nonincumbent: With Opposing Party Holding Seat	14	29
Opposing a Nonincumbent: With Own Party Holding Seat	74	87

SOURCE: Adapted from data in M. C. Cummings, *Congressmen and the Electorate*, (New York: Free Press, 1966), pp. 76–77. Cummings' analysis is based on Presidential election years only. Copyright 1966 by Milton C. Cummings, Jr.

are considerably more likely to defeat other nonincumbents, somewhat more likely to win if their party is winning the Presidency nationally, and considerably more likely to win if the vacated seat was held by their party.

While there may be times and places where incumbency is a disadvantage, the overall pattern indicates a marked advantage. It should be clear then that most congressional seats are not "up for grabs" at each election. Of course, some are. And others, which may not appear to be vulnerable, also are grabbed away. But by and large a senator or representative, once in office, is allowed to stay.

Is the advantage of incumbency diminished by primary elections? The fact is that incumbents enjoy a strong advantage in nomination contests as well as on election day. This holds for Senate and House and for both parties.[17] As shown in Table 2.4, in each of the six elections from 1956 to 1966, more than 85 percent of House incumbents who sought reelection triumphed on election day.[18] It is true that primary fights are more likely in constituencies heavily dominated by one party. The clearest cases are the bitterly contested southern primaries especially in the years when the Demo-

[17] Key, *op. cit.*, pp. 441–450.
[18] Jones, *op. cit.*, pp. 63–68.

TABLE 2.4 Number and Percentage of Incumbents Who Won Reelection, 1956 to 1966

YEAR	TOTAL INCUMBENTS SEEKING REELECTION	THOSE WHO LOST THE PRIMARY		THOSE WHO LOST THE GENERAL ELECTION		THOSE WHO WERE REELECTED	
1956	411	6	1.5%	16	3.9%	389	94.6%
1958	394	3	0.8	37	9.4	358	89.8
1960	403	5	1.2	26	6.5	372	92.3
1962	393	11	2.8	14	3.6	368	93.6
1964	397	8	2.0	44	11.1	345	86.9
1966	407	5	1.2	40	9.8	362	89.0

SOURCE: Charles Jones, *Every Second Year* (Washington, D.C.: Brookings Institute, 1967), p. 68.

cratic nomination was tantamount to election. Also all senators or representatives would prefer to avoid primary fights, which consume energy, time, and money needed for the election compaign. Even the threat of such a battle may be sufficient reason for incumbents to keep their fences mended and party activists happy back home. But considered from the standpoint of selection to Congress, the proposition stands. Once in office, most senators and representatives are allowed to stay.

CANDIDATES AND ISSUES

There is an old American adage: "Vote the Man, not the Party." Indeed, one ideal democratic model of the voter imagines him as balancing both candidates' personal attributes and positions on the issues and then deciding for whom to vote. While there are comparatively few such model voters, in some elections candidates and/or issues may be decisive. One may best look for this phenomenon in the exceptions to the patterns sketched above: where minority-party candidates win despite traditional party loyalties, where they win despite a strong Presidential vote for the other party, or where nonincumbents defeat incumbents.

National issues sometimes become salient at the state or district level and affect a campaign. The Eisenhower administration's farm policies and declining agricultural prices, combined with nonpartisan droughts, "dislodged" a number of prairie-state House Republican incumbents in the late 1950s, even some who had conspicuously voted against the Eisenhower program. A Presidential policy was construed as a partisan issue in the campaign, and this issue hurt Republican congressmen. Senate campaigns in the 1950s featured charges of Communism, particularly against incumbents. At times even the Presidential candidate can become a local issue. Many Republicans went to considerable lengths in their 1964 campaigns to disassociate themselves from the Goldwater ticket on the well-founded assumption that the "Goldwater issue" would affect Republican congressional fortunes.[19]

Local issues sometimes make the difference. The story is told of the 1952 campaign in the normally Republican First District of Kansas, where GOP Representative Albert Cole was running for re-election. Cole's district included several cities on the Kansas River, which had suffered severely from summer 1951 floods. He had voted in Congress to authorize construction of a flood-control dam in the district. The issue polarized First District voters into prodam townspeople and antidam farmers whose farms would be inundated. This situation inspired the candidacy of Democrat and soil conservationist Howard Miller whose campaign was "End Big Dam Foolishness."[20] The antidam farmers prevailed, and Kansas sent its first Democrats to the House. Miller won, it can be noted, despite traditional party loyalties and a strong Eisenhower vote and against an incumbent. (Two years later, the Republicans regained the seat with a new candidate, William Avery, who ran on an antidam platform.)

A candidate's personal attributes also may be decisive. Voting cues may come from race, religion, ethnic background, statewide reputation, hints of scandal, and marriage or divorce. Widows of congressmen have constituted almost the sole source of women in the House of Representatives. Presumably the parties urge widows to

[19] For some effects of the "Goldwater issue" on congressional elections, see Robert A. Schoenberger, "Campaign Strategy and Party Loyalty . . . ," *American Political Science Review*, LXIII (June 1969): 515–520.

[20] Cummings, *op. cit.*, p. 65.

run rather than perhaps more experienced professionals because it is believed that the candidate's name and a sympathy vote will influence the election. Indeed, widowhood seems the most acceptable marital status to the voter. Divorce is political suicide; bachelors are suspect; and marriage was responsible for the one Democratic seat the Republicans managed to capture in 1958. Coya Knutson was the incumbent Democrat from Minnesota's Ninth District. As Key tells it, her husband was somehow gulled into making the plea, "Coya, come home," which the Republicans adopted as a campaign theme. The Republicans won.[21]

The candidate himself may have been the major "issue" in the 1968 Oregon senatorial race. The incumbent, Wayne Morse, 68, was challenged by Republican Robert Packwood, 35. A well-known maverick, Morse had started his Senate career as a Republican, then had served as an Independent for three years, and finally had become a Democrat in 1955. Through all the changes in party, he had been reelected by the Oregon voters. Morse's strong opposition to the Vietnam War evidently was not a major issue; Packwood also had taken a dovish stand. The Republican nominee stressed age difference and the fact that Morse's maverick career had hurt Oregon. According to Packwood:

When Morse went to the Senate in 1944, Oregon was third from the top among Western states in the amount of money received from the Federal Government compared to the amount the government collected in taxes. Today in 1968, we are at the bottom of the list. Wayne Morse has villified those in the Senate who disagreed with him on any issue so that now, when a reclamation project for Oregon comes up, the other Senators are reluctant to help Wayne out. Oregon just can't afford another six years of Wayne Morse.[22]

Packwood defeated Morse by the narrowest of margins. This is a case where a candidate and his record became an issue. But without survey data, we do not know whether and how the voters perceived the issue. It should also be noted that Morse lost narrowly in a year

[21] Key, op. cit., p. 570. One does wonder what happened when Coya did go home.
[22] Congressional Quarterly Weekly Report, (October 18, 1968): 2797.

when the Presidential tide was not helping Democratic congressional candidates. Nixon also carried Oregon.

A candidate may be defeated through his opponent's positive appeal, although it is more difficult for nonincumbents to project such an appeal than for incumbents. This may have occurred in the 1964 New York senatorial race between incumbent Senator Kenneth Keating and Robert Kennedy. Kennedy's positive image and name—a strong factor any time after 1960, but particularly so the year after his brother's assassination—may well have effected Keating's defeat. However, it is not possible to isolate that factor from the 1964 Presidential vote. Keating was running not only against a Kennedy and a figure of nationwide prominence in his own right, but also running against the Johnson tidal wave.

Clearly, under some circumstances candidates and issues of a particular time and place can make the difference in an election. These are the exceptions, the "festivals" of the political culture. *Visibility* may be one common factor in these cases—a visibility, or publicity, that gives salience to cues other than party, Presidential choice, or incumbency. Only a very visible event cuts through to the voters' "threshold of awareness" of congressional affairs. Usually the event is negative—something big enough and *bad* enough to shatter the high tolerance level for things-as-they-are. An issue highly salient to the electorate may have its own visibility. No one has to work very hard at creating an issue if there is one foot of water in the voters' living rooms. But visibility can be produced through other means as well. Much of an incumbent's advantage may reduce to the fact that of the two candidates he is the one whose name is even known. Because visibility may be a key factor in exceptional elections, the campaign devices used to achieve it assume considerable importance.

THE CAMPAIGN

The overall strategy of any campaign for political office is to reinforce existing support, activate latent support, and, if possible, convert some of the opponent's support. But as all realistic campaigners know, hoped-for conversion cannot be the mainstay of a campaign. Those in the game agree that people's minds resist change. Even if new issues and images are projected, selective exposure, selective perception, and selective retention will tend against opinion change. Given certain predispositions about politics, people tend not to expose themselves to sources that contradict their political predispositions. Democrats are apt not to read political editorials in a Republican newspaper. Second, even if exposed, selective perception serves to screen out contradictory impulses. Voters are more likely to see the "good side" of the candidate whom they already favor. And finally, even if some of the bad side is perceived, this "information" will be retained a shorter time than favorable items. The same tendencies work at the other extreme. Those most strongly in support of the candidate need little reinforcement. As one campaign manager has summed up the problem: "Those who are the easiest to reach are the most difficult to change."[23]

By and large, the thrust of campaign energies is directed at activating and crystallizing latent support—at trying to "reach" those who are not easy to reach. Publicity is crucial. Face-to-face contacts, such as "coffees" and speaking engagements; media advertising, through billboards and newspapers, radio and television; general and special mailings; house-to-house and telephone canvasses: all are directed at least in part to this end. While a majority of senators and some representatives, especially those in competitive districts, hire professionals in public relations and advertising, congressmen and managers stress the importance of volunteer help and the candidate's personal organization.[24]

---

[23] Conrad F. Joyner, "Running a Congressional Campaign," in Cornelius P. Cotter (ed.), *Practical Politics in the United States*, (Boston: Allyn & Bacon, 1969), p. 164.

[24] For the best of the campaign literature, see Clapp, *op. cit.*, pp. 373–443; Lewis Froman, "A Realistic Approach to Campaign Strategies and Tactics," in M. Kent Jennings and L. Harmon Zeigler (eds.), *The Electoral Process*, (Englewood Cliffs, N.J.: Prentice-Hall, 1966), pp. 1–20; Charles Jones, "The Role of the Campaign in Congressional Politics," in Jennings and Zeigler (eds.), *The Electoral Process*, pp. 21–41; David Leuthold, *Electioneering in a Democracy* (New York: Wiley, 1968); and Stanley Kelley, Jr., *Professional Public Relations and Political Power* (Baltimore, Md.: Johns Hopkins Press, 1956).

Support for all that campaign energy comes from three major sources, whose relative importance varies with the candidate's particular situation and his political environment. First, there is the party organization at the local, state, and national levels and the congressional campaign committees, which are affiliated with the national party committees. Congressional campaign committees are maintained by both parties in the Senate and the House. However, such congressmen complain that the party organization is not much help. As one veteran House Democrat put it:

> I don't think there is any element of the party that is particularly interested in or concerned with the election of members of Congress. The National Committee is preoccupied with the White House and the state committee has its eyes on the state house and the county committee is interested only in the court house. The congressman is just sort of a fifth wheel on the whole wagon.[25]

Certainly, the amount of party support appears to vary considerably from candidate to candidate. Thus Abraham Ribicoff's 1962 senatorial campaign in Connecticut relied heavily on the state organization, received $15,000 (out of an estimated $230,000 spent) from the Democratic Senate Campaign Committee, and was buttressed by President Kennedy, who visited the state three times to stress that he needed Ribicoff's vote in the Senate. For contrast, consider the 1964 reelection bid of Minnesota Republican Representative Clark MacGregor. He not only had to rely heavily on an elaborate volunteer organization, but also had to try to *avoid* association with the national Republican party.[26]

Second, there are nonparty groups, some well-established and fairly permanent, others formed for one election or one issue. Such groups may proffer financial support, general publicity, or mailings to the members of a special-interest group. Well-known nonparty groups include the AFL-CIO's COPE (Committee on Political Education), ADA (the liberal-oriented Americans for Democratic Ac-

[25] Clapp, *op. cit.*, pp. 397–398.
[26] John Bibby and Roger Davison, *On Capitol Hill* (New York: Holt, Rinehart & Winston, 1967), pp. 30–71.

tion), and the conservative ACA (Americans for Constitutional Action). In 1963, business groups organized BIPAC (Business-Industry Political Action Committee) to counter labor and liberal influence and to provide financial aid for candidates "who support sound fiscal policies and who uphold the free, private, and competitive system."

And third, there is the candidates' personal organization and personal contacts. Because parties and nonparty groups must spread their support across a number of candidates, it is the personal organization—the candidate's own contacts for money, talent, workers—that bears the major burden of the campaign effort.

Within this context of the importance of publicity and the need for resources to reach the voters, the incumbent's advantage can be more clearly seen. Representatives echo the maxim, "Elections are won in the off year." The publicity inherent in the office, the assistance of a trained staff, free mailing privileges, the opportunity to build goodwill while in office—all give the incumbent a tremendous headstart. The size of this advantage over the most hard-campaigning challenger is suggested by a survey in which respondents were equally as able to identify the name of the incumbent in a non-contested contest as in a contested election.[27]

One question deserves careful attention. If incumbents are regularly reelected, and if, even without an incumbent in the race, the candidate whose party is strongest in the constituency is usually elected, why is so much effort and money invested in the election campaign? There appear to be two cogent answers. The first is uncertainty. One never is sure of an opponent's strength, the issues that may become salient, or the depths of underlying dissatisfaction in a constituency. As one student of the subject summarizes: "Politicians seldom take elections for granted."[28] The stakes are too high. After all, their job depends on winning. And second, perhaps it helps. Perhaps the energy expended in the campaign and then in office is one main reason for the high incumbency success rate. As

[27] Miller and Stokes, "Party Government and the Saliency of Congress," p. 204.
[28] Clapp, op. cit., p. 428.

Charles Jones notes: "Incumbents sensed, if they did not know for certain, that victory would come if they worked hard until Election Day."[29] This observation can resolve any apparent contradiction between the security of incumbency and the importance of the campaign. Victory would come if they worked hard; the majority of incumbents do not have to run scared, but they have to run.

MARGINAL AND SAFE SEATS

There are, of course, degrees of electoral "safeness." A congressman may repeatedly win by 50.1 to 54 percent of the vote and still feel less than secure about the next election. Presumably he will view that contest differently from his colleagues who repeatedly poll 65 to 90 percent.

How are marginal and safe seats distributed? Table 2.5 presents the distribution of votes, in two off-year elections for all House members and for each region. While the distribution changes from year to year with party and Presidential fortunes and the events of the time, some patterns have held for the past twenty years.

In both elections covered in the table, considerably more than half of the representatives received 60 percent or more of the vote. This safeness is not attributable to the Democratic South, as the regional breakdown makes clear. In the East, Midwest, and West close to 50 percent of the districts are also "safe" by this measure. Looking at the other extreme, if "marginal" is defined as a vote below 55 percent, less than one-fourth of the House is elected from such districts.

"Safeness" has not been only a southern phenomenon. Many safe seats are located in what have been considered "competitive" two party states. In fact, this pattern deserves more careful notice from students of elections. Both parties may elect representatives, but in some districts, there will be little competition. To take an extreme case, in 1962, Massachusetts elected seven Democrats and five Republicans—a fairly even balance. But of the twelve, two were uncontested and eight were elected by more than 60 percent of the

[29] Jones, "The Role of the Campaign in Congressional Politics," p. 29.

TABLE 2.5 Distribution of Congressional Vote, by Region: House of Representatives, 1954 and 1962

1954 DISTRICT PERCENT OF TOTAL VOTE	NUMBER OF REPRESENTATIVES									
	U.S. TOTALS		SOUTH		EAST		MIDWEST		WEST	
60 or more Dem.	172	(40%)	104	(87%)	34	(26%)	23	(18%)	11	(19%)
55–59 Dem.	30	(7%)	4	(3%)	14	(11%)	7	(5%)	5	(9%)
50–54 Dem.	30	(7%)	2	(2%)	10	(8%)	14	(11%)	4	(7%)
50–54 Repub.	63	(14%)	4	(3%)	23	(18%)	23	(18%)	13	(23%)
55–59 Repub.	61	(14%)	3	(3%)	17	(13%)	28	(22%)	13	(23%)
60 or more Repub.	79	(18%)	3	(3%)	31	(24%)	34	(26%)	11	(19%)
Total	435	(100%)	120	(101%)	129	(100%)	129	(100%)	57	(100%)

1962 DISTRICT PERCENT OF TOTAL VOTE	NUMBER OF REPRESENTATIVES									
	U.S. TOTALS		SOUTH		EAST		MIDWEST		WEST	
60 or more Dem.	160	(37%)	78	(70%)	37	(30%)	26	(21%)	19	(28%)
55–59 Dem.	49	(11%)	11	(10%)	19	(16%)	9	(7%)	10	(14%)
50–54 Dem.	39	(9%)	6	(5%)	9	(7%)	13	(10%)	11	(16%)
50–54 Repub.	38	(9%)	8	(7%)	11	(9%)	15	(12%)	4	(6%)
55–59 Repub.	53	(12%)	3	(3%)	20	(16%)	24	(19%)	6	(9%)
60 or more Repub.	88	(21%)	5	(5%)	26	(21%)	38	(30%)	19	(28%)
Total	427	(99%)	111	(100%)	122	(99%)	125	(99%)	69	(101%)

vote. The same pattern holds for the Senate in a number of two-party states: each party has a seat safe for the incumbent. If no region has a monopoly on safeness, neither does any one population type. In 1954, for example, of the 251 safe seats, 81 were considered "metropolitan," 67 were "small town" districts, 61 were "rural," and 42 were "midurban."[30] The metropolitan districts were overwhelmingly Democratic, and the rural districts were overwhelmingly southern and Democratic. It should be noted that there is no clear independent relation between "ruralness" and "safeness" that exists outside of the South. Rural districts in the North were found to be predominantly marginal for Democrats or Republicans.

While the phenomenon of "safeness" is distributed across the nation, it is still possible to identify areas of concentrated party strength. For the past twenty years the Democrats have been able to count on the rural South and the metropolitan East for their core congressional membership, the Republicans on small-town Midwest and East. Thus each party has had districts safe enough to withstand the sweep of an opposing Presidential tide and the battering of national party fortunes, and each party has had a core of regional strength in Congress.

IMPLICATIONS

This chapter has analyzed the effect of congressional elections on (1) the stability of the membership, (2) Congress's capacity to cooperate with and check the President, and (3) the organization's basis in popular control. At this point some preliminary generalizations can be offered.

First, the impact of elections on the stability of the membership should be clear. Party loyalty ensures that the majority of elections will follow lines of traditional party strength. And the electoral advantage enjoyed by incumbents reinforces that stability. Once in office, a congressman is usually allowed to stay. Both party

[30] For definitions and analysis, see *Congressional Quarterly Weekly Report*, (March 30, 1956): 361.

loyalty and incumbency, then, work for the reelection of congressmen and *for a continuation of the existing membership*. The main source of change appears to be the pull of the Presidential vote. A strong Presidential tide may sweep into office a number of congressmen from states and districts in which the President's party is relatively weak. But even in these instances the President's party must have some base of support to pull candidates over the 50 percent mark. The extent and duration of change in membership are further limited by the countertendency of the midterm election. In the absence of "coattails," traditional party loyalties reassert themselves.

The 1968 election offers one of the clearest illustrations of this stability. In a year of volatile emotion, violence, assassination, and war protest, in a year marked by an exceptional third-party candidacy for President and a change in party control of the White House, the Congress stayed serenely the same. Both Senate and House remained under Democratic control, making Nixon the first President since Zachary Taylor in 1848 not to carry his party to victory in at least one house in his initial election. The Republicans gained five seats in the Senate and four in the House. Of 24 incumbent senators seeking reelection, 20 won—for an 83 percent success rate. And of 405 (from a membership of 435) incumbents seeking reelection to the House, 396 won—for a 98 percent success rate. The figures speak for themselves. While some observers see an increase in political interest and in the dissemination of political information through the media, there were no signs in the 1960s of change in the pattern of congressional election results.

Second, elections help shape the boundaries for congressional interaction with the President. Presidential coattails plus the voters' stable party loyalties usually ensure common partisan ground for the President and Congress. With the constitutional staggering of elections Presidents are given in a four-year term a two-year grant of maximum congressional support, with the grant reduced at the midterm election in proportion to the amount initially given. It is part of the standard American treatment of Presidents since 1789. Americans want their Presidents powerful, but they worry about it.

And so they grant power and almost simultaneously take some of the power away.

Finally, these electoral patterns should help clarify the extent and limits of popular influence on congressional action. Much of the influence on elections has little to do with the particular congressman or his actions in Congress. And the congressmen know this. Elections, then, allow a *wide latitude* for congressional behavior. Hence it is to be expected that other participants in the political system will influence congressional behavior. Later chapters will bear this out. And yet, because defeat is always possible and because the voters do control the selection of members, there are *boundaries* to that wide latitude. Public opinion cannot be disregarded by the congressman who wants to keep his job. His confidence in his re-election has one major qualification: victory may be his if he works hard until election day. The area of permissive action is wide, but bounded, and the boundary points can never be fixed with certainty. The implications of this for the activity of "representation" will be explored at length in the following chapter.

Finally, a suggestion for those who are distressed by Congress's resistance to change, or its tendency to cooperate too much or not enough with the President, or the lack of popular influence on policy making. The facts considered here suggest that one key point where "reform" may be initiated is in congressional elections. One factor may account for the advantage enjoyed by incumbents, the Presidential-coattail effect, and party voting: the voters' low level of interest in and information about congressional races. They vote for the incumbent, the party, or the candidate affiliated with the President's party *because they have no strong reason to vote otherwise.* Seen in this light, the 1970 congressional elections—which raised the issues of war and peace, stimulated turnout in some areas, and even inspired a President and Vice-President to join in the fray—may be the first sign of a significant change. If interest is critical, increased public awareness of the importance of congressional elections would alter the stable election patterns outlined here and their effects on congressional action.

CHAPTER 3

REPRESENTATIONAL ROLES

*E*lections tell us much, but we need also to know the congressional-constituency relationship maintained between elections. Only recently has this complex subject been subjected to systematic analysis. We know something of the congressional side, but there is little data on the public's perception of Congress and congressmen. Nevertheless, certain key points of linkage can be investigated. This chapter treats the roles congressmen adopt vis-à-vis their constituents and what they perceive the act of representation to be. It then considers some bases for these roles in communication patterns between congressmen and constituencies and in the congressman's sociopolitical home environment. Hopefully this discussion will at least begin to clarify the extent of popular influence on congressional activity and what can be expected from "representation" in Congress.

Who or what does a congressman believe he represents? A senator may think in terms of his state or a portion of the state or in terms of a national interest. And he may combine them in some way. For example, a senator from Texas acts at one time for the oil interests, at another for "Texas" or "the South," at still another for the national interest. Similarly a representative may look to the district, the state, or the nation or some combination for his representational base. These have been called "areal role orientations," pointing to the geographical area perceived to be represented.[1]

[1] Heinz Eulau *et al.*, "The Role of the Representative," *American Political Science Review* (September 1959): 742–756.

In one attempt to describe the House membership in terms of areal roles, Roger Davidson assigned a sample of representatives in the Eighty-eighth Congress the following proportions:[2]

National orientation	28%
National-district orientation	23%
District orientation	42%

Not surprisingly, district orientation was mentioned most frequently. But it is noteworthy that as many as 28 percent of the representatives sampled expressed a national view of representation.

The existence of multiple areal roles is particularly important for the Senate. Here is a small group of men elected to serve in a national assembly—to advise and consent on matters of gravest national concern, particularly foreign policy. Yet each is elected from one state. Senator X is the *United States* Senator from Michigan or Massachusetts or Mississippi. The phrasing is so well accepted that the representational dilemma it poses is scarcely appreciated. Tariffs to protect a state-based industry or a freer trade policy for the nation? Articulate a state's view on civil rights or support the President's view of a national interest at stake in the issue? The list is almost endless. One of the major charges leveled against the Congress is the parochialism that gives individual state and local interests primacy over the national interest. And one of the major arguments of those who seek to restrict the congressional scope is that the Presidency is the one office that can speak for a national interest. The conflict of areal roles is built in by the Constitution, and each Senator—and the Senate as a twentieth-century institution—must try to come to terms with it.

Congressmen also differ in their perceptions of the representational relationship, particularly in how they view the role of representing. Three major roles can be identified:

Trustee: The representative perceives his relationship as substantially nonbinding. He will act in Congress according to his own judgment of

---

[2] Roger Davidson, *The Role of the Congressman* (New York: Pegasus, 1969), p. 122. The other 8 percent could not be placed in any of the three categories.

issues at stake or the problems involved. He does not look to the constituency for instructions, nor necessarily follow any he might receive. He acts for the represented in the sense that he follows what *he* believes their best interest to be.

Delegate: The representative perceives his relationship as substantially binding when clear "instructions" exist and requiring at minimum consultation with constituents to see if such instructions are forthcoming. He acts for the represented by following what he perceives *they* want him to do.

Combined-Type or "Politico": The representative has no firm commitment to either of the above roles, but perceives his relationship as varying with the political necessities of the situation. He may consult his constituency and act in accord with his perception of their wishes or he may disregard these wishes and follow his own judgment on certain issues. He acts for the representative in either of the ways outlined above but he decides which way depending on *his* judgment of the situation.[3]

While few congressmen are "pure" delegates or trustees, and thus in a sense all may be "politicos," such a classification provides a useful differentiation among tendencies. In the first, the focus is on the congressman; in the second, on the constituency; in the third, it fluctuates between the two.

A study of the House Agriculture Committee by Charles Jones found both that members take one or another of the three roles in committee deliberations and that some members act in different roles at different stages of the same legislation. Congressmen seem well aware that independent judgment—or the role of trustee—must be used on a number of issues because they have better information than the constituency. Said one:

I am sent here as a representative of 600,000 people. They are supposed to be voting on all the legislation. I try to follow my constituents— to ignore them would be a breach of trust—but I use my judgment often because they are misinformed. I know that they would vote as I do if they had the facts that I have. A lot of people expect you to use your judgment.

Another explained quite clearly how his role as representative might vary with the legislation being considered:

[3] Eulau, *op. cit.*

I thought that it [the agriculture bill under consideration] was a good bill and then I thought that I could go ahead in view of the referendum and support the bill. . . . On some legislation I hear from the people and rely on their judgment. . . . On labor legislation I rely on groups in my area since I don't know too much about it.[4]

This flexibility in roles also was found by Davidson. Representatives in his sample were distributed as follows:[5]

Trustees	28%
Delegates	23%
Politicos	46%

Nearly half articulated the combined "politico" role. They could, depending on circumstances, go either way.

Other varieties of role perceptions in their effect on committee activity, party support, and relations with the President will be discussed later. But the discussion to this point should make clear the varieties of "representation" which are occurring in Congress. Roles vary with the congressman and with the issue.

The importance of issue to type of representation deserves elaboration. Warren Miller and Donald Stokes' pilot study indicates that the degree of fit between (1) constituency opinion, (2) congressional perception of constituency opinion, and (3) congressional activity varies considerably with the kind of issue.[6] The three issue areas investigated included some of the past three decades' most controversial policy questions. One was approval of government activity in the social welfare field, including issues of public housing, public power, aid to education, and the government's role in maintaining full employment. A second was support for American involvement in foreign affairs—particularly foreign economic aid, foreign military aid, sending troops abroad, and aid to neutrals. A third was approval of federal action to protect civil rights. The congruence of attitude between congressman and constituency was strongest on civil rights,

[4] Charles Jones, *Every Second Year* (Washington, D.C.: Brookings Institution, 1967), pp. 365, 366.

[5] Davidson, *op cit.*, p. 117.

[6] Warren Miller and Donald Stokes, "Constituency Influence in Congress," in Angus Campbell *et al.* (eds.), *Elections and the Political Order* (New York: John Wiley, 1967), pp. 351–372.

weaker on social welfare questions, and virtually nonexistent on foreign policy. To take the extreme cases, clearly no representation-by-instruction takes place on foreign policy questions. Wherever the congressman looks for cues about foreign policy decisions—whether to the President, to colleagues, or to his own judgment—it is not to the constituency. He acts *for* them. He is guided by what he believes (or is persuaded to believe) his constituents' best interest to be. On civil rights, however, constituency attitude correlated highly both with the representative's perception of its attitude and with his attitude as expressed in questionnaires and roll call votes. This does not necessarily imply that the constituency in any way directly instructs him. The correlation undoubtedly reflects, at least in part, the fact that congressman and constituency are influenced by the same social environment and hence are likely to share many beliefs and attitudes. But it does imply the same kind of representation suggested by the delegate role in which a representative acts for the represented by following what he perceives they want him to do. He may also independently want to act this way. The point is there exists on civil rights in contrast to the other issues examined a correspondence between what both want to be done.

Miller and Stokes conclude that

No single tradition of representation fully accords with the realities of American legislative politics. . . . Variations in the representative relation are most likely to occur as we move from one policy domain to another. No single, generalized configuration of attitudes and perceptions links Representative with constituency but rather several distinct patterns, and which of them is invoked depends very much on the issue involved.[7]

Why does type of representation vary with the issue concerned? One of the significant variables probably is the *salience* of an issue to the constituency. Kansans may care little about urban housing programs or aid to India, but very much about farm price supports. The citizens of Oregon's Second Congressional District may care little about price supports, but very much about a proposed dam or the closing of a nearby air base. And the voters of Arkansas' Fifth

7 *Ibid.*, p. 371.

Congressional District evidently cared very much about Brooks Hayes' "moderate" stand on civil rights. In most constituencies probably only one or two issues are of intense concern, with most other questions provoking various shades of indifference. Following this reasoning, one could then identify "interested" and "indifferent" constituencies on any one issue[8] and determine whether patterns of representation vary according to level of interest.

Consider, for example, post-World War II farm policy, particularly such questions as price supports and parity levels, production controls, commodity credit, and the like. There was a clear party split, which emerged early in the New Deal. The Democratic party asserted that it is in the national interest for the federal government to support agriculture. As one Manhattan Democrat argued: "The further away from the land we go, the weaker we become, and the closer to the soil we stay the stronger we get."[9] The Republican party opposed such support as "giveaway programs." In the words of one Republican congressman: "In the name of consumer sense stop this indefensible destruction of our liberties and follow the lead of President Eisenhower out of the wilderness of surpluses, waste, and disgusting dependence on the Government for a dole and back to the common virtues of industry and thrift that made our State and Nation great."[10] Note the problem for Republican congressmen from "interested" farm districts. To vote with the party would be to vote against constituency interest. Democrats from "interested" districts had no such problem: party and constituency were in accord on this issue. David Mayhew analyzed roll call votes on major farm legislation from 1947 through 1962. (See Table 3.1.) Democrats, whether from interested or indifferent districts, supported their party's stand on farm policy. But Republicans from interested districts did not support their party. As Mayhew points out: "The record on roll calls during the sixteen postwar years was one of persistent defection from party ranks by Republican farm congressmen on farm

[8] The terminology is David Mayhew's, from his *Party Loyalty Among Congressmen* (Cambridge: Harvard University Press, 1966).

[9] *Ibid.*, p. 12.

[10] *Ibid.*, p. 39.

TABLE 3.1 Votes of Farm and Nonfarm Congressmen of Each Party on Six Important Farm Roll Calls, 1947–1962

| | | VOTES | | | |
| | | DEMOCRATS | | REPUBLICANS | |
YEAR	ISSUE	FARM	NON-FARM	FARM	NON-FARM
1947	Vote to recede from House Conference position, to override Republican leadership and restore A.A.A. soil conservation funds.	62–0	98–1	25–24	18–162
1952	Vote to extend 90% of parity program for basic commodities	57–4	90–44	33–2	42–49
1954	Substitution of Benson 82.5% of parity program for House Agriculture Committee's 90% program	2–69	44–87	19–19	172–5
1956	Passage of Administration-opposed high parity program	69–2	124–33	25–12	25–139
1958	Attempt to suspend the rules and pass Senate omnibus bill as amended by House Agriculture Committee	70–6	117–35	20–11	22–142
1961	Vote on President Kennedy's omnibus farm program (modified)	68–3	117–58	24–8	28–114

SOURCE: David Mayhew, *Party Loyalty Among Congressmen* (Cambridge: Harvard University Press, 1966), p. 30.

issues."[11] And the likelihood of defection increased with the percentage of constituents involved in farm work: "The more farmers a Republican congressman represented the more disposed he was to desert his party on farm votes."[12]

[11] *Ibid.,* p. 43.
[12] *Ibid.,* p. 40.

In this case, the interests of the district were clear enough for a large number of Republican farm congressmen to go against party pressure and vote with the Democrats. And the clearer the interest— that is, the larger the percentage of farmers the congressman was representing—the more he was likely to defect from party to represent home interests.

Mayhew found the same pattern for legislation of major importance to the cities: mainly votes on federal rent control, urban renewal, and subsidized public housing programs. While there was some interparty consensus on urban renewal programs, at least by the time of the Eisenhower administration, the parties still differed in their relative support for urban programs. The Democrats managed to speak not only for farmers but also, with some smooth political legerdemain for the cities. Republican Jacob Javits, then a Representative, addressed a very pointed argument to his party shortly after the 1948 election. He spoke for rent control in the name of "some 70 Republican Members who came from big cities and who are not here today. Those men want to run again, they want to be elected, and I think we on our side have to give some thought to their situation."[13] On a number of issues Republican congressmen had the unpleasant alternatives of voting against the party or against their constituency's interest. And again, it was mostly Republicans from interested districts who defected from party. Where clear constituency interests can be identified, congressmen tend to act for that interest, even when they must vote against the party to do so.

Salience, it seems, is a key factor affecting the congruence of attitude between congressmen and their constituencies. Representation varies with issues as concern for the issue varies. To return to the Miller-Stokes' findings, although few constituencies have spoken with one clear strong voice on questions of foreign aid, many—particularly in the South—have been very clear about the federal government's role in civil rights. What appears to be representation in Congress, then, is a varied pattern of action at least partially linked to constituent interest. Congressmen may or may not communicate

---

[13] *Congressional Record* (March 11, 1949): 2286; cited by Mayhew, p. 70.

with constituents on a question, but in determining this there has been the prior "communication" expressing whether the question is or is not of great concern. Needless to say, such prior communication need not be explicitly or formally expressed. No Southern rural congressman in certain districts in the late 1950s and early 1960s needed to poll his constituents on civil rights. Nor did the senators and representatives from certain farm states need to count the mail to discover opposition to the Brannan Plan. Seen in this light, those who expect representation to mean congruence of opinion between congressman and constituency on a number of policy questions may be demanding more of the activity than the American voters demand. If on the one or two issues when constituents "care," the congressman acts for them, that may be sufficient.

Roles are based on shared expectations of proper behavior for persons occupying certain positions. And since expectations require some prior communication, we can look to the communication with constituents to help explain what congressmen believe "representation" should be.

COMMUNICATION

Measured by quantity alone, the "communicating" is impressive. Mail—several hundred letters for most offices—is delivered in the House five times a day.[14] Staff members handle most correspondence. If an issue has elicited a large volume of mail, automatic typewriters often are used to produce copies of a standard reply (of course, each letter appears to be an original). In addition, there are special mailings, regular newsletters for constituents, speeches, and press releases sent to home papers and clippings from papers forwarded by the home office. Then there are calls on the Washington office, by constituents, district and state party activists, and representatives of special interests. One representative estimated that during his first two years in Washington there were 13,000 visits

14 Charles Clapp, *The Congressman: His Work as He Sees It* (New York: Anchor, 1964), p. 81; Donald R. Matthews, *U.S. Senators and Their World* (New York: Vintage, 1960), p. 79.

from constituents.[15] For senators and representatives whose home base is near the capital, the pressure of constituent visits is particularly severe. Most congressmen also maintain home offices. And the use of polls is increasing.[16] Obviously, communicating in one or another way with constituents is a large and constant part of congressional life.

However, one kind of communication should be separated from the rest—"service" for individual constituents. People seek advice, favors, information, political position back home, and extrication from bureaucratic red tape. The congressional "service" function consumes most of a staff's working day. This applies particularly to members of the House, who are more approachable, but senators too find that much staff time is devoted to office calls and constituent "errand running."[17] Each plea must be answered. Serious requests must be followed up through casework or staff calls to and on government agencies. Indeed, any consideration of congressional relationships with Executive Department personnel should keep in mind this pressure for constituent service. It is important to a congressman that he or a staff member be able to dial Bureau X or Agency C and get results. Representatives agree that this is the most time-consuming of their jobs and one of the most important. Said one:

> One reason we get the mail is because people either have not been able to find out with whom they should deal or have been exposed to a lot of red tape. The federal government is entering into the lives of people more and more, and the agencies are not known to them or are not near. Thus they think of their congressman. One of the most rewarding things we do is rectifying some of the erroneous decisions or lack of attention from administrative agencies to the problems of individual constituents. In many instances the executive branch is wrong, and the only recourse the individual has is to come to a senator or member of the House.

And another:

> Perhaps in one out of ten instances you can do something. That one case is eminently worth the harassment you give the bureaucracy because

[15] *Ibid.*, p. 76.
[16] Malcolm Jewell and Samuel Patterson, *The Legislative Process in the United States* (New York: Random House, 1966), p. 349.
[17] Matthews, *op. cit.*, pp. 79, 80.

it is a way of cutting across the veritable bureaucratic chain. It is worthwhile politically too.[18]

One way to "represent" a constituency, then, is to serve the personal interests of a large number of *individual constituents*. But this has little to do with the other congressional business, carried on in committee or on the floor or in consultation with colleagues and staff— of shaping government policy.

To what extent does the communication bear on policy? Do constituents "instruct" congressmen, thus supporting a "delegate" role, which of the three types was found to be the least frequently practiced? On some issues, such as President Nixon's action in Cambodia in the spring of 1970, mail pours into congressional offices. And congressmen are concerned enough to count pros and cons. But such "instruction" is an unreliable exception to the rule. First, on most matters a congressman may encounter no indication of constituency interest. Hence there is no viewpoint to represent. Second, even if there has been some comment on a subject, a senator or representative may not perceive it as an issue back home. How is a certain amount of mail pro or con to be interpreted? To what extent is the letter-writing minority representative of the constituency? A congressman may employ questionnaires or polls to determine the silent majority's attitudes on a subject, but such an expenditure presupposes the issue was already perceived to be a possible concern. And finally, even with clear constituency interest, other questions must be answered before it can be concluded that "instruction" has occurred. What does the congressman hear? How is he likely to interpret it?

Lewis Dexter points up some of the problems. A congressman hears most often from those who agree with him. His relationship with his constituency is apt to be maintained through a small and, typically, homogeneous group of individuals whom he knew before election or has come to work with since. Further, a congressman's reputation among those who wish to influence him may determine

18 Clapp, *op. cit.*, pp. 86, 87.

what is actually said to him. Accordingly, communication on issues tends to be in the direction of congressional predispositions. Further, what a congressman hears may be interpreted in a number of ways. Dexter cites the case of two representatives from similar districts in the same city. One said he did not hear much about foreign imports. The second reported that it was the first or second most important issue in his district, the other being unemployment.[19] Both "heard" about unemployment, according to Dexter, but only one linked the district employment problem to the issue of trade. Communication also may be interpreted differently at different times. As one senatorial assistant explained:

I've seen it a dozen times. One time some letter or call will come in from "Minersville" and nobody will pay any attention to it. They might say, for instance, the miners are all worried about this foreign fuel oil. Another time a call will come in in the same words almost and everybody will get worried as hell about it; it might be that the State Chairman was in the day before and says, "We're not doing so well in 'Coal County' so we all jump to the conclusion that its fuel oil that is hurting us there. Or it may be just accident; one time the Senator is preoccupied, another in a relaxed mood, but the third time he listens eagerly. You know how it is.[20]

But to put these problems of communication in perspective, one must remember that many senators and representatives feel strongly that they "know" the constituency's wishes, intuitively, because they have "lived there." Charles Jones' study of House Agriculture Committee members showed such intuitive "communication" was the most frequently cited way of determining constituency wishes, with personal contact second and correspondence third. Consider one typical explanation for reliance on this political sixth sense:

You are in a position to know, of course, on a lot of things. I live there— there are many things I just know, I don't have to ask anybody. There

[19] Lewis Dexter, "The Representative and His District," in Robert L. Peabody and Nelson W. Polsby (eds.), New Perspectives on the House of Representatives (2nd ed.; Chicago: Rand-McNally, 1969), pp. 11, 12.
[20] Ibid., p. 21.

are very few bills where I have to guess. If I did, I wouldn't be here as representative.[21]

Belief in this intuitive understanding of constituency needs clearly reduces in importance other sources of communication.

Communication on legislative questions, then, is erratic, partial, and subject to variation with the issue and the time. This pattern helps explain the importance of flexible representational behavior, as embodied in the role of "politico," and the fact that few congressmen embrace the role of "delegate." If a congressman receives comparatively few "instructions" from his constituency, he need not feel that following such instructions is central to appropriate representational behavior.

ATTENTIVE CONSTITUENTS

Each congressman represents an attentive and a general public. As Ralph Huitt points out:

[The congressman] responds to *different* constituencies on different issues. He may try to paint an image of himself in the broadest strokes as an "economiser," say, for the vast number of voters who will try to remember *something* about him when they go to the polls, while at the same time he works to amend one line of a bill to please a half-dozen labor leaders who can make or break him by the kind of voter-registration effort they put on. These are "constituencies"—the people of varying degrees of influence, knowledge, and intensity of feeling who are aware of and respond to particular issues.[22]

Attentive constituents are individuals or groups, within or outside the party, who both know and care a great deal about what happens in Congress. Not only have they "read or heard something" about both candidates, but also a number of them make it part of their business to read and hear, especially about incumbents. Political activists can make life relatively pleasant or unpleasant for congress-

[21] Charles Jones, "Representation in Congress: The Case of the House Agriculture Committee," *American Political Science Review*, 55 (June 1961): 366.

[22] Ralph Huitt, "Congress: The Durable Partner," in Ralph Huitt and Robert L. Peabody (eds.), (New York: Harper & Row, 1969), p. 228. Italics in original.

men. At times, they can even defeat them. Huitt mentions labor's well-known promise and/or threat to mount a voter registration drive. Groups and individuals can give or withhold campaign funds. Primary fights may be threatened. Attentive publics count enough to be listened to, and in the absence of "any word" from a broader public, they may be the constituency that is heeded.

Not enough is known about the relationship between congressmen, attentive public, and general public. Apparently, a considerable amount of congressional activity is devoted to these attentive publics. One study of a state legislature bears out the expectation that in terms of education level and occupational status attentive constituents resemble legislators more than either resembles the general public, that they are listened to by legislators, and that they perceive themselves as playing an active role in political life. The authors of the study conclude that attentive publics may serve to "link" legislator and general public.[23] But another possibility is that they may substitute for the general public. These are the people back home whom the legislator talks with and hears from and depends on to interpret political situations. These are the people who provide the personal contacts that congressmen rely on as explicit sources of information. They also are the people who care about specific legislation and are in positions to affect the congressman's next bid for reelection.

More research is needed on the role of attentive publics, but it seems clear that a major part of the job of representing must be construed in such specific terms. Interest in political life, as in much of human activity, brings its own influence. Things are more likely to be done for those who are watching.

LOBBYISTS

The institutionalization of such attentiveness is called lobbying. The Lobbying Act of 1946, which was passed as part of the Legislative Reorganiaztion Act, requires that any individual or group that

---

[23] G. R. Boynton, Samuel C. Patterson, and Ronald D. Hedlund, "The Missing Links in Legislative Politics: Attentive Constituents," *Journal of Politics*, 31 (August 1969): 700–721.

"solicits, collects or receives money or any other thing of value to be used principally to aid in . . . the passage or defeat of any legislation by the Congress of the United States" must register his name and report his spending. Court interpretation of the act has limited its application to those who engage in direct communication with members of Congress. As of 1965, approximately 8000 individuals and organizations had filed reports. Lobbying is clearly a major activity on the congressional scene. Indeed, as noted by a House committee, it is a "billion dollar industry."[24] Organized groups do more than try to influence congressmen. Often they are the initiators of proposals for legislation, and they may even help write it. Congressmen may look to such groups for information about issues and voter interest, and thus regular patterns of legislator-lobbyist relations are developed. All admit that this is part of the legislative process.

The public image of the corrupt and powerful lobbyist may explain why some overestimate lobbying as an exertion of *pressure* on an otherwise unwilling congressmen. Recent studies suggest that the lobbyist's visibility to the legislator may be weaker than is commonly thought, that lobbyists tend to work with already sympathetic congressmen, that lobbyists often participate with legislators in the give-and-take of managing conflict, and that the legislator-lobbyist relationship is by no means a one-way communication of influence. A special-interest group is not likely to work to defeat a usually sympathetic senator who may have voted "wrong" twice during a six-year term. Lobbyists need the goodwill of congressmen at least as much if not more than the congressmen need lobbyists. An antagonized legislator can be deaf to future pleas or, in extreme cases, threaten a congressional investigation.[25] As two students of the legislative process conclude:

[24] House Select Committee on Lobbying Activities, Eighty-first Congress, 2nd Session, *General Interim Report*, p. 8, cited by Matthews, *op. cit.*, p. 177.

[25] Useful recent summaries of lobbying activity can be found in Lester Milbraith, *The Washington Lobbyists* (Skokie, Ill.: Rand McNally, 1963); Lewis Dexter, *How Organizations are Represented in Washington* (Indianapolis: Bobbs-Merrill, 1969), and "The Representative and his District"; Jewell and Patterson, *op. cit.*, pp. 277–298.

Lobbying activity is, in the main, directed at legislators who sympathize with the policy positions of the group or groups involved; lobbyists depend very substantially on their friends—those who sympathize with their cause. Much of lobbying involves the reinforcement and activation of sympathetic legislators, rather than the conversion of legislators from one policy position to another.[26]

One reason congressmen may perceive as little "pressure" as they say they do may be the contemporary practice of casting the relationship in terms of friendly exchanges of information by two at least partially sympathetic political participants.[27] Further, legislators are, characteristically, loquacious. In any communication between legislator and lobbyist, chances are the lobbyist will do as much listening as talking.

REASONS FOR REPRESENTATION

One final point needs clarification to complete the analysis of representational roles. Lack of interest explains why congressmen feel free to look elsewhere for cues. But what persuades congressmen to follow the constituency on salient issues? What are the reasons for representing?

A traditional argument for party competition is that it encourages the officeholder to be responsible to the electorate. He acts for his constituency because he must face that constituency in the next election. Without competition, then, there is no such threat and no need to represent constituents interests. Typically, more than half of the senators and representatives from both parties are elected by 60 percent or more of the vote. Incumbents typically win reelection. Does this mean that these congressmen will be less likely to represent their constituents than their more electorally vulnerable colleagues? Is it competition that makes a congressman representative?

There is no clear answer to the question. It is argued, for example, that congressmen from electorally marginal districts will exhibit

[26] Jewell and Patterson, op. cit., pp. 297, 298.
[27] Matthews, op. cit., p. 178.

weaker party loyalty in roll call votes than their safer colleagues. When party and constituency are in conflict on an issue, congressmen are more likely to defect from party. There is some slight evidence both for and against this hypothesis.[28] But it can be said that aggregate analysis has not established a clear relationship between congressional ' voting behavior and past levels of electoral competition. Even on specific kinds of issues, evidence of the impact of competition, which is measured by past election results, is meager. Mayhew compared party loyalty on city issues for Republican urban congressmen he had categorized by median GOP electoral percentage. Because these Republican Representatives were subject to conflicting pressures, it was assumed that a low party loyalty score would reflect voting for the constituency. But there was no clear difference between the party loyalty of congressmen from marginal districts (51.6 to 55.4 percent GOP) and that of those from less competitive districts (55.7 to 59.0 percent GOP) or from still safer districts (59.3 to 70.7 percent GOP). Yet Mayhew does point out that other considerations may blur the impact of competition—for example, that "one way for a Republican to construct a safe seat in a city area was to vote with the Democrats on city questions."[29]

Part of the difficulty in proving the impact of electoral competition may come from the assumptions made and the measures used. A seat won by 60 percent or more is traditionally called "safe," but a congressman may view it differently depending on his optimism—or pessimism—and *act* as if his were a marginal district. Investigators use past election results to measure safeness, but within one term a situation may develop that changes political realities. One drought or one drop in farm prices and one unpopular Secretary of Agriculture may rapidly reduce a safe district to very marginal status. Indeed, a number of "safe" Republican constituencies that won persist-

---

[28] For lack of positive evidence, see Froman's analysis of the Eighty-seventh Congress (First Session) in *Congressmen and Their Constituencies* (Skokie, Ill.: Rand McNally, 1963), pp. 111-121. For some positive evidence from the Eighty-sixth and Eighty-seventh congresses, see Wayne Shannon, "Electoral Margins and Voting Behavior in the House of Representatives," *Journal of Politics*, 30 (November 1968): 1028–1045.

[29] Mayhew, *op. cit.*, pp. 76–78.

ently with more than 60 percent of the vote suddenly elected Democrats in 1958. Further, investigators use congressional roll calls to measure the activity of representing a district, but there are other, less easily measured ways a congressman can seem to act for his constituency. Congressmen can act one way in committee and another on the floor.[30] A Republican congressman, who represented Utah ranchers, delivered a speech—which filled a full page of the Congressional Record—in behalf of an amendment to include grazing lands in the soil bank program and then voted with the party leadership against the amendment.[31] Arguments that competition affects congressional behavior assume congressmen perceive that they must act in a certain way to ensure reelection. And yet the indicators used for competition do not necessarily measure that perception.[32]

In another attempt to study the question, Davidson related electoral competition to representational roles with some interesting preliminary results. He found that marginal-seat congressmen were more likely to view themselves as delegates than trustees and to take a district-oriented rather than a national view. Safe-seat congressmen (those elected with 60 percent or more of the vote in the last election) tended to be nationally oriented and to be trustees.[33] This relationship needs to be corroborated by further analysis. But it suggests that electoral competition does affect congressional views of representation. (Whether it accounts for observable differences in actions is still unanswered.) And it suggests also that safe-seat members may perform an important function in congressional representation: they are permitted the luxury of taking the more "statesmanlike," national view.

Certainly, there are many examples of action that apparently is dictated by concern with electoral vulnerability. Congressmen often

[30] Jones, op. cit., pp. 358–367.

[31] Ibid., p. 43.

[32] For a first step in this direction, see John W. Kingdon, "The Study of Legislative Voting: Review and Original Research," a paper delivered at the Annual Meeting of the American Political Science Association, New York, September, 1969.

[33] Roger Davidson, The Role of the Congressman (New York: Pegasus, 1969), pp. 117–129.

desert the party leadership on the grounds that to vote with them could "hurt him back home." Such instances are cited so frequently that it is difficult to believe they do not reflect some reality. The question is still open. But what may be said at this point is that the very unclearness of the pattern strongly suggests that competition is not the *only* factor influencing the results. Congressmen may represent their districts from other motives than the threat of election defeat.

A second reason for representation undoubtedly is the influence of the environment shared by congressman and constituency. The Constitution specifies that congressmen must be residents of the states and districts they represent. State and local party organizations tend to discourage the newcomer or the outsider from making a bid for office, even if he meets the residence requirement. Both factors combine to produce a membership that, although significantly higher in educational level and occupational status, shares many of the beliefs and attitudes of the folks back home. As pointed out before, congressmen take pride in intuitively knowing—and serving —the needs of their constituencies. This, no doubt, contributes to the often-criticized congressional "parochialism," an insistence (rooted in constitutional reasoning and honored in twentieth-century practice) that the "Virginian" or "Californian" or "Tenth District" view on an issue must be represented.

The most dramatic example in the past two decades of defection from party is provided by southern Democrats, many of whom had never experienced a contested general election. Even southerners with little to fear from primary contests deserted the national party to represent their states' views on civil rights. While the threat of reprisal on election day cannot be discounted completely, it seems likely that deep-rooted beliefs—the product of the socialization they and their constituents had experienced—dictated southern Senators' filibuster against civil rights legislation and vote against the national government's "assault" on "states' rights."

A third reason for representation may be, quite simply, that the congressman *wants* to represent. It is what he is there to do. This attitude is reflected in all explanations of role, whether it be that of delegate or trustee or some combination of the two. How he votes, which committees he chooses—whatever he does—the congressman usually explains in terms of the activity of representing. Of course, the reason cited may not be the real motive. But the fact that it is cited suggests the strength of the norm. Congressmen, according to the congressional view, are supposed to represent.

Thus the combined effect of three factors may explain why a congressman's actions are consonant with his constituency's attitudes about salient issues: the threat of defeat in primary or general election, shared beliefs and attitudes, and his perception of the congressional role as one that prescribes representation. This combination of influences explains why competitiveness alone does not appear strongly related to constituency representation. Even safe-seat congressmen have reason to defect from party or to ignore other pressures in favor of the constituency.

SUMMARY

Communication between congressmen and their constituents is erratic and partial and varies greatly from issue to issue. Congressional roles also vary—in terms of both what is considered the constituency being represented and in what the activity of representation means. When party and constituency are in conflict, congressmen are more likely to defect from party. Taken together, these points delineate no single and one-dimensional pattern of representation in Congress, but rather a complex pattern of linkage, which is both variable and partial. The interests represented in different ways in one session may not be represented at other times or in other ways.

This pattern can help interpret the congressional election results outlined in the preceding chapter. Voters tolerate a wide, though finite, latitude in congressional activity. If something "bad" enough occurs, incumbents may be defeated, but in most times and places they are returned to office. This chapter points also to a wide latitude for congressional discretion in the continuing relationship between congressman and constituency. Only very limited "instructions" are given the congressman by his constituency—even by his attentive constituency. Outside of that area of concern, he exercises his discretion on the wide range of legislation before the Congress. This chapter also helps interpret the widespread electoral safeness noted in Chapter 2. One cannot assume that safe-seat congressmen will be less willing to "represent" their constituencies than their colleagues from marginal seats. First, the constituency does not ask that much in the way of representation. And second, shared attitudes and beliefs and the congressman's desire to be representative help explain why even the safest, most entrenched incumbent may rarely disappoint his constituency.

Because pressure from the constituency is not that firm, continuing, or demanding, other influences—from within Congress and from without—can have a decisive impact on congressional activity. These will be considered in the next chapters.

CHAPTER 4

NORMS AND THE DISTRIBUTION
OF INFLUENCE

*L*egislatures, like other human organizations, are social systems characterized by stable patterns of action and by widely shared standards of what that action should be. These standards are norms. Norms are informal rules, frequently unspoken because they need not be spoken, which may govern conduct more effectively than any written rule. They prescribe "how things are done around here." Norms are by no means phenomena peripheral to the social system. They are part of its core structure—they develop out of the system's needs and, in helping resolve them, perpetuate and extend certain system characteristics. In this way they are analogous to the structure of beliefs, inhibitions and role definitions, that helps define an individual's "character." That structure is partly a product of past action and experience and partly a contribution to future action. The analogy points up the importance of norms as (1) an *influence* on social action and (2) a *linkage* between past and future action. They prescribe how things ought to be done (in the future). But implicit in the prescription is the power to prescribe. Thus norms are also descriptions of power in the past and present—how things have been done, how they are being done. As such, they constitute a structure important for understanding the social system at any one point in time and a dynamic for understanding its change or lack of change over time.

Norms may be of particular importance for the study of Congress. First, as explained earlier, unlike many organizations and groups,

Congress cannot control the selection of its own members. Through a selection system an organization can systematically choose and eliminate attributes and thus ensure group cohesiveness and conformity to certain goals. But a democratic assembly is permitted no such selectivity. True, the American party system performs some prior "screening" of the congressional membership. It recruits men already active in state and local politics and who are skilled in compromise. It discourages the amateur, the unknown, the rigidly doctrinaire. It screens out women, some ethnic minorities depending on the locale, and the unusually mobile. However, there still exists considerable variation across the nation in those the party system "passes." Without the aid of a deliberate systematic selection from within the Congress, norms must carry the burden of socialization. Norms must ensure group cohesiveness and conformity to organization goals.

Second, the stability of the congressional membership through the twentieth century indicates particularly favorable conditions for the development of norms. A stable membership provides not only sufficient time for the development of stable, widely shared standards of action, but also sufficient influence for old members in the socialization of new members.

And third, norms imply power—power to prescribe future action. They are therefore crucial to understanding a political institution faced with the problem of organizing power.

This chapter accordingly concentrates on congressional norms: what they are, why they exist (that is, in what way they contribute to institutional needs), and what their political import may be.

CONGRESSIONAL NORMS

In the late 1950s, Donald Matthews described the "folkways" of the Senate, drawing on past impressionistic accounts by insiders privy to Senate life and his own more systematic interviewing.[1]

[1] Donald Matthews, "The Folkways of the United Senate: Conformity to Group Norms and Legislative Effectiveness," *American Political Science Review*, (December 1959): 1064–1089.

Later studies indicate closely parallel norms at work in the House.[2] The point to notice is that congressmen themselves both can articulate these norms and are in considerable agreement about them. It is also important to note the similarity between the two chambers. The Senate and House could develop different norms, different degrees of observing them, or the same norms. Further research might well explore possible differences. But the present account treats four major norms found in both Senate and House. Together they shed considerable light on the congressional institution.

SENIORITY

One major norm governing congressional behavior is that of seniority. Freshman senators and representatives are expected to be fairly unobtrusive,[3] to do their homework, and not to take too noticeable a part in floor debate. They receive the leftover committee assignments and office space. In committee meetings and hearings they sit at the end of the table—and speak last. Recent congresses appear to have relaxed such constraints somewhat. And freshmen are beginning to play a fuller, more responsible role. According to Charles Clapp: "Freshmen are now advised to defer speaking only until the moment arrives when they have something significant to say."[4] Yet influence and deference still belong to those who have been there longest.

It has been argued that freshmen representatives are subject to somewhat greater restraint than freshmen senators since the smaller number of senators and the greater prestige of the office may permit a broader range of Senate behavior. Certainly the freshman senator is more visible than the first-term House member. And it is true that the new senator is almost immediately handed a subcommittee chairmanship, which in the larger House may take three or four

[2] See Richard Fenno, "The Internal Distribution of Influence: The House," in David Truman (ed.), *The Congress and America's Future* (Englewood Cliffs, N.J.: Prentice-Hall, 1965), pp. 52–76; and Charles Clapp, *The Congressman: His Work as He Sees It* (New York: Anchor, 1964), pp. 9–55.

[3] Matthews, *op. cit.*, p. 1065.

[4] Clapp, *op. cit.*, pp. 12, 13.

terms to win. But it should be noted that such a comparison, however plausible, requires more exact measurement of the operation of the norm in the two chambers. Here, as with so many of the alleged Senate-House differences, no serious comparative research has been undertaken.

The other side of the freshman's plight is the senior's advantage. Senior senators enjoy committee influence, can dominate floor debate, and usually are given first choice in committee transfers. The same holds true for the House. Richard Fenno describes the norms that "superintend the House career of every member" as the *seniority-protégé-apprentice system:*

> Seniority rules rest on the basic assumption that a man must first spend time learning to be a representative, just as he learns any other occupation. Seniority signifies experience, and experience brings that combination of subject-matter knowledge and political wisdom which alone is held to qualify a man for leadership in the House. Before a member can be certified as an experienced senior member, he must first be an apprentice and a protégé.[5]

The norm of seniority distributes influence in both House and Senate unequally by length of service, but predictably. Predictability may be its greatest attraction to junior as well as senior members. Those who have most to gain from the norm—the seniors—are in a position to reinforce the norm. Those who have less to gain can count on predictability—and take the long view.

SPECIALIZATION

A second major norm governing congressional activity is specialization. Senators and representatives should not try to talk on all subjects. They should not even expect to have opinions on all subjects. Congressmen are urged to specialize—presumably in some area of their committee work. They should carve out their own area of knowledge, do their homework, and stay out of other areas. This norm applies to senior as well as junior members, excluding only party leaders, who are charged with scheduling, managing, and

5 Fenno, *op. cit.,* p. 71.

integrating of the full burden of congressional business. From specialization comes influence. Wilbur Mills, chairman of the House Ways and Means Committee, speaks with the most powerful voice on tax legislation in Congress—in part because of his seniority and the chairmanship (to which he succeeded through seniority) but also because he is believed to know more about tax legislation than any other man in the House. The norm applies to floor speaking. Said one senator: "The really effective senators are those who speak only on the subjects they have been dealing with at close quarters, not those who are on their feet on almost every subject all the time."[6] And it applies to accepting other congressmen's opinions. The noncommittee member will rely on the judgment of experts on the committee.

RECIPROCITY AND ACCOMMODATION

From specialization comes the norm of reciprocity, which may be expressed in a number of ways: "You support my legislation and I'll support yours." "I'll listen to you on housing and you listen to me on feed grains." Or as one congressman put it: "I won't be an S.O.B. if you won't be one."[7] Basic to the norm—whether its implementation involves trading votes, bargaining for favors, or tacitly agreeing not to disrupt another member's legislation—is accommodation, each to the other's specialization and/or constituency concern. Note that the word "logrolling" (reciprocal voting for each other's bills) has unpleasant connotations in American public opinion, but in Congress the mutual aid of which logrolling is one kind is considered *proper* conduct. Members are expected to "play the game" when their constituents' immediate concerns are not involved. Reciprocity is thus part of the larger, all pervasive norms of compromise and negotiation.[8]

These norms apply even at the committee and subcommittee levels, although not on all committees. A committee can be considered a social system with a discernible structure of norms gov-

[6] Matthews, *op. cit.*, p. 1068.
[7] *Ibid.*, p. 1072; see also Fenno, *op. cit.*, pp. 75, 76; and Clapp, *op. cit.*, p. 15.
[8] Fenno, *op. cit.*, pp. 75, 76.

erning its activity. The House Appropriations Committee, for example, requires specialization. The individual usually specializes in one of the subcommittees he is assigned to—and may even specialize *within* a subcommittee on the work of one agency or program. For example, the Subcommittee on Agriculture of the House Appropriations Committee has included one specialist in the work of the Extension Service and the Farmers Home Administration, one specialist in the Forest Service, one in soil conservation, and one in the school lunch and meat inspection programs. The Appropriations Committee also requires reciprocity. Since committee members defer to each other's expertise as specialists, decision-making is based on subcommittee autonomy and mutual respect. As one member explained: "It's frowned upon if you offer an amendment in the full committee if you are on the subcommittee"; "Also it's considered presumptuous to pose as an expert if you aren't on the subcommittee." The result is that subcommittee decisions are usually accepted by the full committee (whose decisions in turn are usually accepted by the House). According to members' estimates, subcommittee recommendations "go smiling through," "are very rarely changed," "almost always approved," "changed one time in fifty." Negotiation and compromise take place in the subcommittee, where members give and take until they can achieve a unanimous recommendation. The influence that accrues to a subcommittee through such norms is obvious.[9]

All committees do not reinforce these particular norms, but the fact that they *are* carried to the committee stage, and to such a powerful committee as Appropriations, suggests something of their strength and pervasiveness.

INSTITUTIONAL LOYALTY

Congress, as any ongoing institution, requires loyalty to the institution itself. Members are expected to be loyal to the Congress and to the House and Senate, respectively. At times this norm may cause conflict between the two chambers. Who wins how often in a

[9] Fenno, *The Power of the Purse* (Boston: Little, Brown, 1966), pp. 160–167, 209–219.

conference committee? Which chairman goes to the other chairman's office for negotiation? These questions can become sore points in Senate-House relations. But the norm also prescribes congressional loyalty vis-à-vis the Executive Branch and, most importantly, dictates that no issue is important enough to destroy the chamber. Senator Joseph McCarthy was censured by his colleagues in 1954, not so much because he had indiscriminately labeled individuals as Communists or because he had abused the congressional power of investigation. He was censured because he had attacked the integrity of the Senate. Institutional loyalty also helps explain why such censures are so rare. Congressmen will rally to protect the reputation of colleagues in order to protect the name of the institution of which they are a part.

There are other norms shared by the House and Senate. The overarching norm of compromise was mentioned only in passing, and the norms of party loyalty will be treated later.

SANCTIONS

In any social system, sanctions may be invoked against the maverick, the person who does not conform to group norms. Sanctions may take the form of group disapproval. After he had completed a floor speech, one freshman Democrat was told by senior Senator George of Georgia, that "Freshmen didn't use to talk so much." And it was difficult for William Proxmire to serve an "unobtrusive apprenticeship" during his first year in the Senate. The "word" was quickly passed on. As Ralph Huitt tells it:

The warnings were characteristic of the operations of the Senate. None of them was direct. They came in friendly tips; someone heard an unnamed person say it, the report was passed on to a Proxmire staff man for what it was worth. Or a very senior senator in the chair would pointedly overlook Proxmire standing at his desk, to recognize other members ahead of him out of turn.[10]

Sanctions may also take the form of reduced influence. Congressmen unwilling to limit themselves to one area specialization may find that

[10] Ralph Huitt, "The Outsider in the Senate: An Alternative Role," in *Congress: Two Decades of Analysis* (New York: Harper & Row, 1969), p. 166.

they are not listened to even in their specialization. Congressmen who refuse to be accommodating find few willing to accommodate them. Such sanctions are no minor matter. Group approval is highly valued in a stable membership where colleagues must work with each other for some time to come. And influence is the currency by which these political men must live.

Of course, some congressmen do deviate from the norms. As Ralph Huitt argues, the role of maverick is a legitimate and viable Senate role to adopt. When Proxmire found unobtrusiveness and "going along" psychologically impossible, he became a self-admitted maverick. The senators who were concerned about his early floor speaking has seen nothing yet. In June of his first Senate year, he offered six amendments to the Mutual Security Act and pressed them to a vote. (Proxmire was not a member of the Foreign Relations Committee.) Because four of his amendments were first introduced on the floor, the committee could not give them prior consideration. In July, it was social security. He announced his intention "to rise every day, from now on until social security improvement is adopted, to plead for it." He followed through on 27 consecutive occasions. In August, it was water diversion: a bill to allow the Metropolitan Sanitary District of Chicago to increase the amount of water it withdraws from Lake Michigan for a three-year test period. The measure, periodically passed by Congress, was usually vetoed by the President because of difficulties it caused in relations with Canada. Proxmire, who opposed the bill, held the floor from nine to midnight on the last night of the session—until the Senate agreed to defer consideration. So in only three months he managed—conspicuously—to flout the norms of seniority, specialization, and reciprocity. What happened to Proxmire after all this? Huitt argues: "Not much. . . . The Senate is of all official bodies . . . perhaps the most tolerant of individualistic, even eccentric, behavior."[11]

Deviance may be tolerated, but it is not rewarded from within the congressional system. In playing the maverick, Proxmire was foregoing the alternative role of apprentice-protégé, which in time

[11] *Ibid.*, p. 173.

is rewarded with increased influence. It has been noted that the most influential senators are of a "Senate type." They have served their apprenticeship, observed reciprocity, and express deep loyalty to the Senate as an institution.[12] Assignments to the three most prestigious House committees are carefully awarded by the leadership to members who are accommodating and who will not provoke disruptive conflict. Elective leadership positions also tend to be filled by accommodating, institutionally loyal (and senior) congressmen. Influence in the House and Senate, as in any social system, accrues to those who conform most closely to group norms—whose behavior embodies group values.

NORMS AND INSTITUTIONAL "NEEDS"

These norms are by no means unique to the Congress. Any organization needs loyalty to maintain itself. And norms of specialization, accommodation and compromise are found in a variety of social settings. Seniority norms also are widely followed, although Congress is unusual in the degree to which it allows seniority to determine committee influence. But why have these particular norms developed in both House and Senate? Can they be understood in terms of certain "needs" of the congressional institutions?

As was noted in the first chapter, Congress is a representative, collegial assembly which shares with the President the charge of national government. Its characteristics and responsibilities help explain the emergence of these norms. The amount, range, and complexity of legislation it must consider probably dictate the norms of specialization. And the constitutionally built-in rivalry between the two branches of government further strengthens the norm. Most congressmen are professional politicians, but comparatively few arrive as experts in specific subject matter areas. Specialization permits members to gain expertise, which Congress must be able to assert in its dealings with the administration. If Appropriations Committee members are to achieve their goal of "guarding the

---

[12] For a good description of this phenomenon, see William S. White, *Citadel, The Story of the U.S. Senate* (Boston: Houghton Mifflin, 1968).

Treasury" against agency onslaughts, they must be well-versed in the agencies and the programs for which appropriations are re quested. And without specialization, and deference to it, each chamber would quickly become mired in the words of 100 and 435 highly verbal men all trying to talk on all subjects.

A norm of reciprocity seems crucial to such a collegial, representative assembly, divided as it is by the claims of individual constituencies and compartmentalized by areas of specialization. Without reciprocity there would be atomization. Individual claims must be translated into corporate decisions, usually by majority vote. Only through reciprocity is majority-building possible. And, as Richard Fenno points out, norms of compromise and accommodation are necessary if an assembly engaged in managing conflict is not to tear itself apart in the process.[13] The norm of seniority also helps reduce conflict by providing an automatic rule for the distribution of influence. It seems especially appropriate for a collegial assembly whose members must, initially, be considered equal. Specialization reinforces seniority. If specialization by committee is important, then the greatest experience in an area becomes the most highly valued. And further, seniority-insured predictability may be of particular importance in an assembly of political men who are interacting with noncongressional political men, who need to know who has and who will have influence over what.

NORMS AND THE DISTRIBUTION OF INFLUENCE

Norms are not neutral. In assigning value to certain actions, they may exert a decisive impact on the organization of influence and on policy. Congressional norms have definite political implications. Specialization and reciprocity strengthen the committee system, reinforce decentralized decision-making, and distribute influence widely through Senate and House. One looks to a few senators on corn, a few others on hogs, still others on housing. Such decentralization of policy-making limits the scope of congressional leadership, as will become clear later, and contributes to a kind of "constituency

[13] Fenno, *op. cit.*, pp. 52–76.

representation" in which congressmen whose constituencies are strongly interested in a certain area attempt to become specialists on the appropriate committee. At the same time these norms work against corporate decision-making: the Senate as a whole does not "deliberate" on agriculture policy. If the "corn" Senators are in agreement, one major part of the "deliberation" has occurred. The norms also counter the more centralized decision-making that occurs through the political parties. Seniority, for example, by distributing influence to members with longest service and strengthening the committee system through the independence it gives the chairmen, further strengthens decentralization and restricts the centralizing effects of party. These norms together help sustain a structure of influence that is decentralized and yet semioligarchical.[14] While many congressmen have influence, some have more than others, and only a few hold sway over a wide range of legislation.

Norms help structure the distribution of influence, but not through a simple one-way process. There is here, as in other such institutions, a complex process of interaction and reinforcement among norms prescribing proper action, patterns of action (such as the distribution of influence), and institutional "needs" or pressures for certain patterns of action. Thus to cut into this complexity at any one point of time, one finds institutional pressures for particular action and particular norms, both of which reinforce each other, which in turn create further pressure for these actions and norms in the future.

An excellent illustration of this complex, mutually reinforcing process is provided by the seniority system. The seniority system is a favorite target for congressional reformers who seem to assume that the restructuring they demand would be a rather simple matter of political engineering. The relationships between the seniority system and other elements in the congressional institution should be analyzed to determine what such reform might entail and, indeed, whether it is practicable.[15]

---

[14] *Ibid.*

[15] The following section draws primarily on an earlier work by the author, *The Seniority System in Congress* (Bloomington: Indiana University Press, 1971).

THE SENIORITY SYSTEM

"Seniority system" refers to the Senate and House practice of ranking committee members, by party, according to years of consecutive service on the committee, thus designating the chairman. The member of the majority party, having longest consecutive service on the committee, automatically becomes chairman. If he leaves the committee, the vacancy is filled by the majority party's next ranking member—and so on down the line. New committee members are added only to the bottom of the party lists. If they choose to stay on the committee, they will automatically climb the seniority ladder. Note that *consecutive* committee service is specified. If a congressman in line for a chairmanship is defeated or retires (for example, to the Vice Presidency) and returns later to Congress and to his former committee, he is placed at the bottom of the list. The seniority system discourages members from making Congress anything less than a full career. Note also that the rule specifies consecutive *committee* service. If a congressman of 15 years' service changes committee, he is placed at the bottom of his new committee's ranking. In this century, the seniority rule has only rarely been violated and then only in exceptional circumstances.

It is the full caucus of the congressionaly party that determines whether there will be exceptions to the seniority rule. Senators Ladd, Brookhart, Frazier, and La Follette were stripped of their committee seniority in 1925 because they had bolted the Republican party in the election of 1924. Senator Morse lost his committee seniority (and his committees) in 1953, after leaving the Republican party and seeking committee assignments as an independent. As the debate on the matter made clear, committee assignments were—and are— considered a party's business. In assigning others to Morse's old positions, the Republicans argued that they were simply following seniority for their party members.[16] Two southern Democrats, John Bell Williams and Albert Watson, were stripped of their House committee seniority in 1965 because they had supported the Repub-

[16] Ralph Huitt, "The Morse Committee Assignment Controversy: A Study in Senate Norms," in *Congress: Two Decades of Analysis*, pp. 113–135.

lican Presidential candidate in 1964. (Neither was in line for a chairmanship. Williams was ranking member behind Oren Harris on Interstate and Foreign Commerce. He left the House to become governor of Mississippi. Watson became a Republican.) The most recent instance, Adam Clayton Powell's deposition from the chairmanship of the House Education Committee, came after Powell not only had supported a Republican Presidential candidate but also, in many observers' eyes, had broken other congressional norms. During the past forty years many others have bolted their party in Presidential elections, but in the face even of such total disloyalty to party, the seniority rule has often held firm. Lesser rebellions against the party and the leadership (such as voting in Congress consistently with the opposing party) have brought no retaliation.

SENIORITY NORM AND SENIORITY SYSTEM

The seniority system, which is adhered to so faithfully, is nowhere mentioned in the formal rules of Congress. It is a customary practice which is strengthened by each year of its observance. This system can be viewed as a *product* of the broader congressional seniority norm previously described. Leadership posts would not be given to the senior committee members unless seniority itself was not considered a valuable congressional attribute. But the seniority system is also a pattern of action which *strengthens* the broader norm by giving it visibility and concrete effect and by giving committee influence to seniors, who will be most suportive of the norm. As the old congressional joke goes: "The longer I'm here the more I like the seniority system."

CONGRESSIONAL "NEEDS" AND THE SENIORITY SYSTEM:
HISTORICAL DEVELOPMENT

The seniority system appeared in both House and Senate in the nineteenth century, a development clearly related to increasing pressures for specialization and the emergence of the standing committees as the major focus for legislative work. It was the Senate that first embraced a full-fledged system. In the House, seniority was one of several criteria for selecting chairmen. Not until the early years of this century, and the weakening of the Speaker's power over committee appointments (1911–1917), did seniority become the single, automatic criterion for selection.[17]

Thus both Senate and House, after experimenting with different systems, opted for relatively decentralized modes of leadership. It can be offered that pressures for decentralization in this collegial assembly would tend to support a *negative* solution to such problems as control over the selection of committee leaders—"negative" here referring to a system which does not consolidate power. The seniority system offers such a solution. By providing an automatic rule for leadership selection, it ensures that no individual or clique will dictate who gets what at this crucial point in the process of distributing influence.

One of the strongest—and oldest—arguments for the seniority system is that "the alternatives would be worse." It points up the essentially negative character of the solution the seniority system provides—the solution not to consolidate power at any one point.

The seniority system is also supported by—and supportive of—another characteristic of Congress: its slowly stabilizing and aging membership. The twentieth century has brought a steadily increasing average years service and a decreasing percentage of new members. It is unlikely that a predominantly junior membership, subject to large influxes of new congressmen, would support a seniority rule. But a senior membership comprised primarily of careerists can see its considerable advantages. Not surprisingly, a sample of Eighty-eighth Congress representatives indicated greater concern with the "problem" of the seniority system the *less* the congressional seniority they possessed.[18] Seniority makes continued service in Congress more attractive. It guarantees automatic advancement and offers predictability over time—a generally highly valued com-

[17] See Nelson Polsby, "The Growth of the Seniority System in the U.S. House of Representatives," *American Political Science Review* (September 1969): 787–807; and Michael Abram and Joseph Cooper, "The Rise of Seniority in the House of Representatives," *Polity* (Fall, 1968), pp. 52–85.

[18] Roger Davidson *et al., Congress in Crisis* (Belmont, Calif.: Wadsworth, 1968), pp. 86, 87.

modity in human society, especially in societies where members plan
to stay. Further with influence decentralized by the committee structure, there are a number of people who have much to gain by a
seniority rule.

The contention that as the membership has become more stable
and older, support for the seniority system has increased is supported by some broad historical indicators. For example, one can determine (in "intervals" of ten Congresses) the mean number of terms
of service of House incumbents since the First Congress, the percentage of committees on which seniority determined choice of
chairmen, and the speakers' mean number of years of prior service.
This is done in Figure 4.1. The graphs indicate a concomitant growth

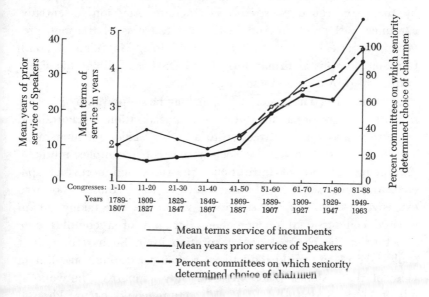

FIGURE 4.1 The Growth of "Seniority" in Membership, Appointment of
Chairmen, and House Leadership

SOURCES: For incumbents and House Speakers, Nelson Polsby, "The Institutionalization of the House of Representatives," *American Political Science Review* (March
1968): 147, 149.

For seniority in chairmanships, Nelson Polsby, "The Growth of the Seniority System
in the U.S. House of Representatives," *American Political Science Review* (September 1967): 792, 793.

of "seniority" in membership, appointment of House chairmen, and House leadership. Of course, they do not "prove" that the seniority of the membership influences support for the seniority system. All three trends may be caused by a yet unidentified factor. But they do provide evidence to support the logic of the relationship as outlined.

In the Ninety-second Congress, both Republican and Democratic caucuses in the House served notice that the seniority rule would not be considered inviolable. Republicans agreed to vote automatically by secret ballot to accept nominations of their ranking minority members. Under the Democratic plan, any Democrat, when backed by ten others, could demand a vote on election of a chairman. But it is not clear that the "changes" brought any real change at all. Assignments in the past had been formally approved by the party caucuses, so the Democratic provision, essentially, continues past practice. And in the first test case of the new provision, the attempt to unseat 72-year-old John McMillan of South Carolina from his chairmanship of the District of Columbia Committee failed by a vote of 126 to 96.

To summarize: The seniority system may be supported by pressure from the congressional institution for specialization, decentralized leadership, and a rule attractive to a stable, senior membership.[19] The seniority system can be seen as part of a complex mutually reinforcing network of institutional pressures and norms of specialization and seniority. If this view is valid, those who urge extensive "reform" of the seniority system are not taking on an isolated congressional phenomenon, but part of a complex core structure of the congressional institution itself. Such reform, if it could take place, would tend to far-reaching repercussions. But in view of the system's place in a strongly supportive network of influences, it is doubtful that such reform could occur. Phrased differently, effecting a substantial change in the seniority system would require such changes in membership, norms, and congression-

[19] Polsby ("The Growth of the Seniority System") concludes similarly that "demands for specialization and routinization," "weak party leadership," and a supportive "large corps of veterans" have contributed to the growth of the seniority system.

al practices that the ensuing congressional revolution would make the seniority change seem minor indeed.

THE SENIORITY SYSTEM AND THE DISTRIBUTION OF INFLUENCE

What are the political consequences of the seniority system? How does it affect the distribution of influence in Senate and House? According to its critics, the seniority system exercises a systematic and far-reaching bias. By rewarding *length of service* the system allegedly gives chairmanships to those from the safest seats, predominantly southerners in the Democratic party and midwesterners and easterners in the Republican party. Because safe seats tend to be rural and their holders "conservative," the system allegedly builds in a safe-rural-conservative bias to the committee leadership. To what extent are these allegations valid?[20]

The earlier discussion of congressional elections casts doubt on one assumption in the argument concerning the "bias" from rewarding length of service. As Chapter 2 made clear, the *predominant* electoral pattern is safeness. And safeness is not an exclusively southern or rural phenomenon. It is enjoyed by approximately 50 percent of congressmen from all regions and population densities. Thus the seniority system rewards length of service in a membership where long service is not the exception but the rule. It might therefore be expected that chairmanships would be distributed more equitably than the critics contend.

Table 4.1 presents a four-part regional summary of percentages of Senate and House members and of chairmen and ranking minority members for the years 1947 through 1966. Compared to the membership in each party, leadership posts are distributed quite equitably for the Republican party and less so, yet approximately proportionately, for the Democratic party. The South is slightly overrepresented for House Democrats; both South and West are

---

[20] For detailed discussion and empirical investigation of the traditional charges against the seniority system, see Hinckley, *The Seniority System in Congress.*

TABLE 4.1 Regional Representation: Committee Chairmen (CC) and Ranking Minority Members (RMM) Compared to All Members: 1947–1966[a]

REGION	DEMOCRATS		REPUBLICANS	
	% ALL MEMBERS	% CC/RMM	% ALL MEMBERS	% CC/RMM
Senate				
East	18	10	38	39
South	42	53	2	1
Midwest	17	3	37	46
West	23	35	23	13
TOTAL	100	101	100	99
House				
East	25	19	36	35
South	45	61	5	1
Midwest	19	14	43	51
West	11	6	15	14
TOTAL	100	100	99	101

[a] All congressmen are counted once for each election won: representatives, from 1946; senators, from 1942.

SOURCE: Barbara Hinckley, *The Seniority System in Congress* (Bloomington: Indiana University Press, 1971), p. 37.

overrepresented for Senate Democrats. The congruence between membership and leadership holds for most of the individual congresses in the twenty-year span. Only by the early 1960s had the South lost its near-majority in Democratic membership but still retained its chairmanships, leading to a southern "bias" in leadership posts. As the table makes clear, the reason for the preponderance of southern Democrats in committee chairs is not so much a "bias" of the seniority system as, simply, the preponderance of southerners in the Democratic congressional membership in that twenty-year span. The pattern holds when regional categories are broken down into individual states. In both parties and in both House and Senate, states receive approximately proportionate numbers of leadership posts depending on the number of Democrats or Republicans they have elected to Congress.[21] Table 4.2 shows the Senate pattern.

[21] *Ibid.*

To investigate a possible bias in policy, one can compare party loyalty scores of the Democratic and Republican congressional membership with those of the committee leadership. The scores measure the percentage of times a congressman voted with his party in Congress when a majority of both parties opposed each other. Low loyalty scores for Democrats indicate conservative voting behavior on roll call votes—that is, behavior closer to that of Republicans. Low loyalty scores for Republicans indicate less conservative voting —that is, behavior closer to that of Democrats.[22]

TABLE 4.2 Members, and Committee Leaders by State: Senate, 1947–1966

	DEMOCRATS		REPUBLICANS	
	SENATORS ELECTED	CC/ RMM	SENATORS ELECTED	CC/ RMM
Alabama	6	1	0	0
Arkansas	6	2	0	0
Georgia	6	2	0	0
Florida	6	0	0	0
Louisiana	6	2	0	0
Mississippi	6	1	0	0
New Mexico	6	3	0	0
N. Carolina	6	1	0	0
Oklahoma	6	3	0	0
Rhode Island	6	2	0	0
S. Carolina	6	2	0	0
Tennessee	6	1	0	0
Texas	6	2	0	0
Virginia	6	2	0	0
Missouri	5	1	1	0
Montana	5	2	1	0
Washington	5	2	1	1
W. Virginia	5	2	1	1
Arizona	4	1	2	1
Minnesota	4	0	2	0
Nevada	4	2	2	1
Oregon	4	0	2	0
Wyoming	4	1	2	0

[22] A strong correlation exists for both parties between party loyalty scores and scores of "liberalism-conservatism," such as scores based on the percentage of times a congressman voted against the conservative coalition. See *ibid.*

TABLE 4.2.—Continued

	DEMOCRATS		REPUBLICANS	
	SENATORS ELECTED	CC/ RMM	SENATORS ELECTED	CC/ RMM
Connecticut	3	0	3	0
Idaho	3	0	3	1
Illinois	3	0	3	2
Kentucky	3	0	3	1
Michigan	3	1	3	1
Ohio	3	0	3	2
Colorado	2	1	4	1
Delaware	2	0	4	3
Indiana	2	0	4	2
Maryland	2	1	4	2
Massachusetts	2	0	4	2
Pennsylvania	2	0	4	1
S. Dakota	2	0	4	2
Wisconsin	2	0	4	3
California	1	0	5	1
Iowa	1	0	5	1
Maine	1	0	5	2
New Jersey	1	0	5	1
New York	1	1	5	1
Utah	1	1	5	1
Kansas	0	0	6	3
Nebraska	0	0	6	3
New Hampshire	0	0	6	3
N. Dakota	0	0	6	1
Vermont	0	0	6	2
Total	164	40	124	46

SOURCE: Barbara Hinckley, *The Seniority System in Congress* (Bloomington: Indiana University Press, 1971), pp. 47–48.

Results for the Senate (Table 4.3), suggest that on this point the critics are partially correct. Both northern and southern Democratic leaders tended to less party loyalty (more conservative voting behavior) than the Democratic membership. However, the Republicans showed no difference in voting behavior between committee leaders and the full membership. An equitable distribution is found for one party and not for the other party.

It appears that the critics have overstated their case for bias.

TABLE 4.3 Party Support: Senate Committee Chairmen (CC) and Ranking Minority Members (RMM) Compared to All Senators, 1955–1966

PARTY SUPPORT SCORE %	ALL MEMBERS %	CC/RMM %
Senate Democrats		
	(N = 285)	(N = 75)
0– 19	1	3
20– 39	10	21
40– 59	18	23
60– 79	48	41
80–100	23	12
	100	100
Senate Northern Democrats		
	(N = 176)	(N = 29)
0– 19	1	0
20– 39	3	3
40– 59	9	28
60– 79	57	52
80–100	31	17
	101	100
Senate Republicans		
	(N = 190)	(N = 72)
0– 19	1	0
20– 39	4	3
40– 59	20	28
60– 79	51	50
80–100	25	20
	101	100

SOURCE: Barbara Hinckley, *The Seniority System in Congress* (Bloomington: University of Indiana Press, 1971), p. 66.

While some conservative bias is observable for the Democrats, basically the seniority system distributes leadership posts in accord with *traditional party strength.* That area or category electing the largest number of Democrats or Republicans to Congress tends to receive the largest number of leadership posts, and so on down the line. Of course, the problem with seniority in some critics' view is that even a few Smiths, Colmers, Byrds, and Eastlands are enough to justify objection to the system that permits them power.

A second effect of the seniority system should be noted. It builds a *time lag* into the process of selecting leaders. Chairmanships are distributed according to the party's numerical strength, but the old, not the new, distribution is reflected in the committee chairs after times of electoral change. The Midwest may elect Democrats to Congress. The South may elect Republicans. But for the next decade, while the new congressmen work their way up the seniority ladder, those regions will have a lesser share of the party's committee leadership posts. The southern decrease in Democratic membership is only now in the 1970s beginning to be felt in the senior ranks. And as urban northern liberals begin to inherit chairmanships, one should not be surprised that attacks against the seniority system come more frequently from conservative (and Republican) members.

Finally, and perhaps most clearly, the seniority system *decentralizes influence* in Congress by providing slots in the committee hierarchy that are secure from outside control. A chairman is secure in his post, and a second-ranking majority member can look forward to the chairmanship, no matter what their disagreements with the party leadership, no matter what their stands on the particular subject matter of the committee's jurisdiction, no matter how weak their party support. The seniority system creates a cadre of leaders independent of the other leadership—the party leadership. By creating this cadre of influential, independent specialists, the seniority system strengthens Congress vis-à-vis the President. Presidents may work through party leaders to push their programs. But against a stubborn and secure chairman, there may be little a President or a party leader can do.

SUMMARY

This chapter has treated major congressional norms. What they are. How they can be understood in terms of institutional pressures. What their political import may be. Deeply rooted in the membership and needs of the congressional institution, these norms form a structure for the distribution of influence. They assert that power shall be decentralized by policy area, that it shall tend primarily to senior, accommodating, compromising men who respect each other's claims and who support the congressional institution. Norms help shape patterns of action through complex, mutually reinforcing relationships such as that between a senior membership, seniority norms, and seniority system. These norms of specialization and seniority are also interlinked with the committee system, which will be examined in the next chapter.

CHAPTER 5

COMMITTEES AND THE DISTRIBUTION
OF INFLUENCE

*T*he major share of legislative business is carried on in the standing committees. This fact, imparted to the freshman upon arrival,[1] is the same fact Woodrow Wilson stressed about the nineteenth-century House:

The House sits . . . to sanction the conclusions of its Committees. . . . It legislates in its committee-rooms; not by the determinations of majorities, but by the resolutions of specially-commissioned minorities; so that it is not far from the truth to say that Congress in session is Congress on public exhibition, whilst Congress in its committee-rooms is Congress at work.[2]

If not "far from the truth," Wilson's description is some distance away. Committees are not fully autonomous decision-making units. Both House and Senate frequently do not sanction committee recommendations. They may be modified or rejected by floor amendments or by the conference committees 'appointed from the House and Senate senior committee members to resolve differences between House and Senate versions of a bill. Further, committees vary considerably in terms of their workload, members' zeal, "minority" character, and influence in the larger arena of Senate or House. Yet it is true that committees provide the fundamental structuring for the

[1] Charles Clapp, *The Congressman: His Work As He Sees It* (Washington, D.C.: Brookings Institution, 1963), p. 13.

[2] Woodrow Wilson, *Congressional Government* (New York: Meridian, 1956 [orig. published, 1885]), p. 69.

division of legislative labor. Legislation is distributed among 21 House and 16 Senate committees, each with jurisdiction in a given area. Influence in that area, accordingly, devolves to the committee members, especially the senior members, and most especially to the chairman.

SUBJECT MATTER: POLITICAL EFFECTS

Committee consideration does not occur in a political vacuum. As a major site for legislative decision, committees may become the nexus of political conflict, as political participants within and without Congress interact with committee members to affect legislation. These other participants, engaged in the primary and persistent interaction with committees, are determined mainly by the subject matter of the committee's jurisdiction. The foreign affairs committees of the House and Senate conduct a major share of their business with the State Department and the Presidential office. The Committee on Veterans Affairs works primarily with a clientele group. Some of the housekeeping committees of Senate and House work primarily with congressional participants. Agriculture committees work with a combination of executive and clientele groups—farmers' groups, specific commodity interests, and agencies in the Department of Agriculture. Committee consideration, then, will vary with the *site of interaction* (that is, executive, clientele, congressional, or some combination of the three). It will vary with the *relationships* established between the committee and these other participants. Committees may be favorable, hostile, or neutral to specific clientele groups or executive agencies. Committees may be looked to with considerable respect or indifference by the House and Senate at large. The amount of respect or indifference will vary with the *extent of interest or controversy* engendered by the subject matter. Legislation provoking congressional controversy may extend the site of interaction to a larger number of participants. Subject matter shapes the relationship between committees and their political environment, and this relationship in turn affects the outcome of legislation.

It is important to note the stability of these relationships, at least throughout the tenure of one chairman. Committee membership is stable, given the seniority system and the overall stability of congressional membership. Below the level of Assistant Secretary, executive personnel enjoy an equivalent stability. And well-established clientele interests, strong enough to gain access to Congress in the first place, tend similarly to persist over time. Hence stable relationships tend to evolve between committee members and the other participants. Few bills raise wholly new issues. Work on most legislation is viewed as part of a continuing interaction.

This stability has profound effects on policy-making. First, policy-making becomes incremental. Today's decisions are based on what was done yesterday. And the participants can appreciate the precedents because it was they who defined them.

Second, this stability may lead to the formation of what Douglass Cater calls "subgovernments." Subgovernments involve the interlocking, supportive interaction between a congressional committee, an executive agency, and a clientele group. Cater cites among others the case of sugar legislation worked out between Chairman Harold Cooley of the House Agriculture Committee, the director of the Sugar Division in the Agriculture Department, and the Washington representatives of domestic beet and cane sugar growers, refineries, and foreign producers. According to Cater, that tripartite subgovernment set price levels, indirectly influenced United States foreign policy with Latin America, and divided the sugar market to the last "spoonful."[3]

Third, it often serves to inhibit Presidential "innovation." Compared with many congressmen, eight-year Presidents are merely transients. They are only passing through. Legislation on sugar policy or Indian affairs continues as before despite changing occupants of the White House. President Kennedy had to consider Otto Passman, chairman of the House Appropriations Subcommittee on Foreign Aid, as a given in mapping administration aid policy. Kennedy and then Johnson—and the Democratic congressional leader-

[3] Douglas Cater, *Power in Washington* (New York: Random House, 1964), p. 18.

ship—had to work around the Senate Judiciary Committee and the House Rules Committee on civil rights legislation.

COMMITTEE MEMBERSHIP

It follows that congressmen who wish to gain influence in an area will try to be assigned to that committee. Constituency interest is a significant factor. A congressman may seek Armed Services because of a military base in his district, or Agriculture because of local interest in peanuts or wheat. Western senators and representatives traditionally have been drawn to Interior. Other motives of ideology or interest dictate committee choice. Members of the House Internal Security Committee (formerly the Un-American Activities Committee) have tended to be the representatives most concerned with the threat of Communism at home and abroad. And belief in states rights has persuaded southerners to seek membership on the Senate Judiciary Committee. Such self-selection means that likeminded congressmen will tend to move toward the same committees and these committees, then, will tend to exhibit homogeneous points of view.

Some committees have a noticeable regional or ideological character. Western members dominate Interior in both chambers and the Senate Public Works Committee. Southern members dominate Senate Armed Services and House Agriculture and both District of Columbia committees, and eastern and western members, the House Merchant Marine and Fisheries Committee. Committees also vary in their members' conservatism. Although "southern" committees are the most conservative and "eastern" committees the most liberal, ideological character is at least partly independent of the influence of region. The Un-American Activities Committee, for example, is "conservative," but it is not "southern." Both Armed Services committees are conservative" and both Foreign Relations committees are "liberal," but neither has a predominant regional character, producing a striking difference in membership of the committees charged with military policy and foreign policy, respectively.

Other committees, it is clear, cannot be typed in this fashion. Some show no likemindedness at all. Members representing *different* sides of the same issue may be drawn to the same committee, building in a representation of conflicting points of view. "Labor" Democrats and "management" Republicans find their way to the House Education and Labor Committee. Big bank and small bank interests are represented on Banking and Currency. Further, factors other than self-selection figure in the process of committee assignment. A congressman with no views at all about big or small banks may ask for Armed Services and find himself on Banking and Currency, because of the influence of the leadership or the chance of selection. To understand these other factors shaping committee membership, it is necessary to understand the process of committee assignment.

ASSIGNMENT OF MEMBERS

With norms of specialization and seniority applied to the committee system, the particular assignment given will have a profound effect on the individual congressman's career. The committee may be the base for constituency representation. It may also be the route to influence in Congress because some committees are more desirable than others. The House committees on Rules, Appropriations, and Ways and Means—its three most prestigious committees—allow members a wide range of policy influence. At the other extreme are low-prestige committees—for example, Veterans Affairs, Merchant Marine, and House Administration.

There is a clearly discernible committee "pecking order" in both the House and Senate. Variations in prestige are reflected in patterns of transfer from and to committees: members tend to move only from less to more desirable committees. In recent Congresses, for example, the Senate Foreign Relations and Finance committee have been considered among the most desirable, whereas the Post Office and District of Columbia committees were among the least desirable. Similar patterns of preference ranking can be seen in the House, with Rules, Ways and Means, and Appropriations at the top of the prestige ranking and Post Office and Veterans' Affairs at the bottom.

A congressman may gain influence through appointment to a high-prestige committee or he may opt to stay on a low-prestige committee to gain seniority quickly and reap the patronage from a chairmanship of Post Office or become the big fish on Merchant Marine. But a crucial decision must be made in his first two years or so: ask to be transferred at the organization of the next Congress (and lose his committee seniority) or stay on the committee and hope to gain rank quickly? Allocating influence at home and influence in Congress, committee assignments are serious business.

Note the effort some House members expend on securing desired slots. As one described it:

The day after election I called the dean of my delegation and told him my committee preference. He said he would speak to our man on Ways and Means. On the way back from my vacation, I stopped by Bonham, Texas, and spent about five hours there [with Rayburn] and let him lead the conversation. When he asked me what committee I was interested in, I told him. Then I had Adlai Stevenson, the national chairman, and some other people write the Speaker, the Majority Leader, the Whip, and the chairman of Ways and Means in my behalf, and I wrote all of those people myself. Some friends who are close to John McCormack wrote to him and went to see him on my behalf. Another important party leader wrote McCormack and my Ways and Means man about my background, which happened to be appropriate for the committee I wanted.

In addition I phoned some people once I learned they were leaving the committee. I also talked with several other members of Congress whose judgment I valued. Then I called on the committee chairman. I didn't know whether there would be competition for the committee, but I wanted the assignment very much. The process was a great education to me.[4]

All members may not wage such elaborate campaigns, but the general feeling is that some politicking is necessary. According to one observer:

As a minimum, when his party is in the majority, a freshman Democrat should make his committee preference known to the Speaker, the Majority Leader, the Chairman of the Ways and Means Committee, his zone man on Ways and Means, and the chairman of any committee in which he is interested.[5]

[4] Clapp, *op. cit.* pp. 223, 224.
[5] *Ibid.*, p. 221.

He might also contact all others of his party on Ways and Means, the party whip, and the dean of the state delegation. The process for Republicans is similarly intricate.

Although the mechanics differ, the process is essentially the same in the House and Senate. Each congressional party appoints a committee on committees whose recommendations are submitted to the full party caucus for ratification. On each committee a certain number of seats are available to each party (the number varies with committee size, party ratios vis-à-vis the full membership, how many members seek transfers, and the size of the freshman class.

Democrats on the House Ways and Means Committee serve as their party's committee on committees. Goodwin determined that the committee was regionally and ideologically representative through ten congresses (Table 5.1), but that it was comprised primarily of senior and safe-seat congressmen. For example, in the Ninetieth Congress, only two committee members had won the past election with less than 60 percent of the vote. Freshmen rarely are appointed to Ways and Means.[6] House Republicans appoint a separate committee on committees, with one member from each state that has a Republican in the House. Each member has as many votes on the committee as there are Republicans in his state delegation. This gives large and heavily Republican states the advantage. In the Ninetieth Congress, seven states had 50 percent of the votes on the Republican committee on committees: California, Illinois, Michigan, Ohio, New Jersey, New York, and Pennsylvania.[7] The Senate Republican Committee on Committees has been regionally and ideologically representative and has recruited more junior members than its Democratic counterpart.[8] The Senate Democrats' Steering Committee is appointed by the floor leader; members sit for the duration of their congressional service. The committee became more conservative during Lyndon Johnson's tenure as Majority Leader.[9] This

---

[6] George Goodwin, *The Little Legislatures* (Amhurst:· University of Massachusetts Press, 1970), Chap. IV.

[7] *Ibid.*

[8] *Ibid.*

[9] *Ibid.*

was the committee that Senator Clark claimed to be run by the conservative "Senate Establishment." He charged, on the Senate floor, that it used committee assignments to reward and punish members for pro- or anti-Establishment stands in congressional voting. And one pilot study indicates some truth to the charge in that by the end of their first four congresses liberals had received fewer prestigious committee assignments than moderates, and moderates fewer than conservatives.[10] In any event, Johnson's successor, Majority Leader Mike Mansfield, added liberal Democrats to the Steering Committee, including Senator Clark, a case where maverick behavior clearly paid off.

Assignments made by the committees on committees are subject to other influences. Party leaders can have a decisive say in who goes on what committees, as the following rather terrible verse immortalizes:

> I love Speaker Rayburn, his heart is so warm
> And if I love him he'll do me no harm
> So I shan't sass the Speaker one little bitty
> And then I'll wind up on a major committee.[11]

While the House leadership hovers over assignments to the three major committees, it may intervene in other assignments as well. The "dean," or senior member, of a state's House delegation lobbies for his junior colleagues. Interest groups also may try to influence assignments.[12]

In addition, chairmen and ranking minority members have some influence on assignments to their own committees, varying with the issues and personalities involved. There is no formal mode of consultation, but it is evidently common practice for committees on committees to consult with them on potential appointees. Hopeful members pay courtesy calls on prospective chairmen. The general feeling is that in some cases strongly positive and in most cases

[10] Wayne Swanson, "Committee Assignments and the Nonconformist Legislature," *Midwest Journal of Political Science,* (February 1969): 84.

[11] Quoted by Arthur Krock, *New York Times,* April 8, 1958.

[12] Nicholas Masters, "Committee Assignments in The House of Representatives," *American Political Science Review* (June 1961): 345–357.

strongly negative reactions by the senior member will be respected. As one member of the House Republican Committee on Committees expressed it:

I don't see how the Committee on Committees could have the nerve to ram somebody down the throat of a committee chairman or ranking member who doesn't want that candidate. It would be natural to consult with your top man on the committee, and unless some unusual issue is at stake, his wishes would be adhered to.[13]

This informal veto power, to the extent it is exercised, is important. It offers one additional means for ensuring continuation of a committee's distinctive character and views on issues and one additional barrier against change.

CRITERIA

According to congressmen who have been interviewed, the most important criterion applied is to assign congressmen to committees that will help toward their reelection.[14] Since it is doubtful that congressmen from marginal districts receive preference in consideration over congressmen from safe seats, perhaps the criterion should be restated as one of "constituency representation." Where possible, congressmen are given committees whose jurisdiction corresponds to a constituency interest—westerners go to Interior, eastern coast representatives to Merchant Marine, and so forth. Congressional seniority is a second criterion. A desired slot usually will be filled by a congressman seeking transfer, not by a freshman: the more senior the congressman the better his chance for assignment. Some committees follow the "same-state" rule: when a member dies or retires, his seat is given to a congressman from the same state. Thus Ohio claims a permanent seat on the House Public Works Committee. Ways and Means follows this rule for its Democratic appointees,[15] as does the House Armed Services Committee. Some committees add special criteria of their own. The House Education and

[13] Clapp, *op. cit.*, p. 220.
[14] Masters, *op. cit.*, pp. 345–357.
[15] John Manley, *The Politics of Finance* (Boston: Little, Brown, 1970), p. 43.

Labor Committee traditionally included labor-oriented Democrats and management-oriented Republicans, a Roman Catholic (who presumably would support aid to parochial schools), and some southerners who presumably would oppose integration of schools). Notice the conflict built into that committee by the patterns of assignment. Liberal and conservative, spokesmen for labor and for management, segregationist, and sectarian advocates are tossed in together, and—as if with a "Go to it, boys!"—the battle is on. There has been no likemindedness on the House Education and Labor Committee. The point to note is that committee unity or conflict may be built in by a systematic process of assignment.

The three major House committees have their own criteria for membership, which is applied by the party leadership. According to Nicholas Masters, members of Appropriations, Rules, and Ways and Means:

. . . are selected by the party leaders in consultation with the members of the committee on committees, rather than the other way around. A nominee's name may be first brought up by the party leaders, a committee member, or even by someone not involved with the mechanics, but whatever the technical circumstances surrounding the introduction of his name, if the nominee is assigned, he bears the party leaders' stamp of approval.[16]

This applies to both parties. The leadership selects members who are "responsible legislators"—who are able to compromise and accommodate different points of view. They should respect congressional norms. They tend to be from safe districts (it is argued that a safe congressman, less constrained by constituency demands, is better able to compromise on controversial matters). They will be senior. And they will be geographically representative of the congressional party.[17] (As noted above, House Democrats apply the same-state rule when filling Ways and Means vacancies.)

Committee assignments, then, comprise an intricate and critical part of the process of distributing influence. They reinforce major congressional norms (seniority and legislative "responsibility") and

[16] Masters, *op. cit.*, p. 352.
[17] *Ibid.*, pp. 345-357.

further the continuation of traditional policies and ways of conduct-ing business. Members are encouraged to stay on committees by the seniority system. And when transfers and new assignments are made, committee identity tends to be perpetuated through self-selection, the same-state rule, the specific criteria applied for that committee, and the influence of the chairman. At the same time they offer a structure for constituency representation, which permits a number of congressmen to work in the specialized policy area of major concern to their constituencies. And by the different criteria applied, assignments build in different types of membership. Com-mittees vary according to members' consensus on goals or tasks, prestige and stability, and legislative orientation—that is, whether they are "responsible legislators."[18] This variation in membership, it will be seen, affects the committee's influence in the full house and influences the site where legislative decisions are made.

THE CHAIRMEN

The particular characteristics of the membership are important because most committee decisions are made by majority vote. But one committee member stands out in importance. That is the chair-man. His powers are impressive. He schedules hearings, calls meet-ings, appoints subcommittees and their chairmen, deploys the com-mittee staff, and influences who will speak in floor consideration and who attends conference committees. His goodwill is prized by members seeking a present or future subcommittee chair. Protected by the seniority system, he is independent of the party leadership.

These powers can be employed to facilitate or to obstruct con-gressional action, with the most publicized cases involving obstruc-tion. Chairmen may decide not to schedule hearings or not to hold meetings when legislation they do not favor is before the committee. In the Ninetieth Congress more than half the committees had no

[18] These are four of the five characteristics Richard Fenno isolates as con-tributing to committee "integration." The fifth is subject matter, treated above. See Richard Fenno, "The House Appropriations Committee as a Political Sys-tem," *American Political Science Review* (June 1962): 310–324.

regularly scheduled meeting days but met "at the call of the chairman." Rules Chairman Howard Smith was home in Virginia inspecting a "burned barn" for some time after the 1957 Civil Rights Act legislation reached his committee. And in the late 1950s, when an education bill was on the House Education and Labor Committee's agenda, months would slip by before Chairman Graham Barden would call the next meeting. He used his procedural power to terminate meetings by declaring the absence of a quorum. Once to protract hearings, he summoned 92 witnesses from the Chamber of Commerce and was going to let them all talk.[19] Chairmen, further, may choose not to hire large staffs, which severely limits the committee's capacity to oversee administration.

In addition, subcommittees can be manipulated for specific policy objectives. When A. Willis Robertson, Chairman of the Senate Banking and Currency Committee and strongly protective of Federal Reserve policies, discovered that committee members Clark and Proxmire planned to use a subcommittee to investigate specific Federal Reserve action, he simply abolished the subcommittee. Federal Reserve business was then handled in the full committee— with Robertson as chairman. Senate Labor Committee Chairman Lister Hill reportedly found that problems of the aging, which were within the purview of his committee, interfered with his good relations with the American Medical Association. He exiled the subject to a new subcommittee in the Eighty-sixth Congress. (In the Eighty-seventh Congress, it was banished still farther from Hill's jurisdiction —to a select Senate committee.)

Chairmen, however, are by no means "czars" of their committees. A majority of members can act, although admittedly they have more power on some committee than on others. And there have been revolts in which majorities have mobilized to wrest power from a chairman. Graham Barden was relieved of some command in the Eighty-sixth Congress. Members of the House Government Opera-

---

[19] Richard Fenno, "The House of Representatives and Federal Aid to Education," in Robert L. Peabody and Nelson W. Polsby (eds.), *New Perspectives on the House of Representatives,* (2d ed.; Chicago: Rand-McNally, 1969), p. 299.

tions Committee mutinied against Chairman Clare Hoffman in the Eighty-third Congress. They voted virtual autonomy to subcommittees, giving each the power to appoint staff and fix their pay, to subpoena witnesses, and to hold hearings outside Washington. (Hoffman has been described as a loner with few legislative friends, who had antagonized Eisenhower and other Republicans, had not consulted the Democratic ranking minority member on committee business, and had made great use of ad hoc subcommittees whose creation and membership were under his discretion.[20]) In the liberal Eighty-ninth Congress, Post Office and Civil Service Committee members rebelled against conservative Chairman Tom Murray of Tennessee and voted rules that limited his choice of subcommittee chairmen and members, his discretion in referring matters to subcommittees, and his control over budget and staff.

There have been few such revolts. But their possibility and the norm of cooperation between chairmen and members help define the limits within which chairmen operate and thus restrict any clearly arbitrary rule. Observers agree that "one-man rule" is atypical,[21] and that the most influential chairmen are those who keep close to their majorities.[22]

One of the best illustrations of the point is provided by Wilbur Mills, Chairman of the House Ways and Means Committee. Both Democratic and Republican members agree that Mills "runs" the committee, but that he runs it by seeking consensus. He will "compromise, bargain, cajole, swap, bend, plead, amend, coax, and unite until as much of the controversy as possible is drained from the bill, and as many members of the Committee as possible support it."[23] Mills' influence appears closely connected with his and the members' perception that he is accountable to them. John Manley summarizes the basis of Mills' influence: "The decisions of the Committee are

[20] Goodwin, op. cit., pp. 61, 62.

[21] See, for example, Stewart Udall, "A Defense of the Seniority System," New York Times Magazine (January 13, 1957): 17 ff.

[22] Charles Jones, "Joseph G. Cannon and Howard W. Smith . . . ," Journal of Politics, (August 1968): 618.

[23] John Manley, "Wilbur Mills: A Study in Congressional Influence," American Political Science Review (June 1969): 445.

shapod and aiticulated by Mills, but if his word comes close to being law in the Committee it is because he has listened well to the words of others."[24]

Again, one needs to keep in mind the committee-by-committee variation in the power of chairmen. At present, committee rules differ widely, giving some chairmen more prerogatives than others. Some committees make extensive use of their subcommittees; others conduct their business mainly in full committee and under the chairman's watchful eye. Chairmen differ also in leadership style and in the informal prestige they wield within Congress and within the committee. Representative Richard Bolling's description of various House chairmen supplies one insider's insight into variations in prestige. Bolling frankly names chairmen of considerable power— Howard Smith of Rules, Wilbur Mills of Ways and Means, Carl Vinson of Armed Services—and chairmen who had little power even in their own committees. Liberal Emanuel Celler, claims Bolling, never really "ruled" his more conservative committee. Second-ranking "Tad" Walter of Pennsylvania wielded more influence. And Bolling tells the story of Adolph Sabath of Illinois, one-time Rules chairman, who "was trying to make himself heard at a meeting of his own committee." Finally, ranking Republican Les Allen of Illinois conceded grandly: "Adolph has a right to be heard. Let him speak for two or three minutes."[25]

In sum, through their individual prestige, leadership style, relationship to the committee's majority, and policy views, chairmen can exercise an independent impact on the committee's decisions.

COMMITTEES IN THE LEGISLATIVE PROCESS

Committee consideration is an initial and frequently decisive stage in the legislative process. Upon submission in either house, bills are immediately referred to the relevant committee for study and recommendation. Committees or their subcommittees will hold hearings

[24] *Ibid.*, pp. 442–464.
[25] Richard Bolling, *House Out of Order* (New York: Dutton, 1966), pp. 79–115, especially p. 83.

on the proposed legislation, inviting opinions of interest-group representatives, outside "experts," and Executive Department personnel. Staff members study practical or political implications. Hearings may provide the opportunity for representation of different interests, although chairmen have been known to "pack" the hearings with spokesmen for one point of view. After the hearings, the committee meets in executive session. It may add amendments or delete provisions or it may rewrite the entire bill or parts of it. On a favorable majority vote, the committee version of the bill is reported out. A minority report may be filed—explaining objections, suggesting amendments, and such. Committees rarely report bills with negative recommendations. They report them favorably or in amended form, or they do not report them at all. House bills face the additional obstacle of the Rules Committee which is discussed at length later.

There are then six major stages at which a bill may be stopped. The Senate or House standing committee may refuse to report it, as may the Rules Committee. If it passes these three, it may still be defeated on the Senate or House floor or in a conference committee. A bill requires support at all six stages. Five is not good enough. In the legislative game, it's all or not at all.

If a hostile standing committee attempts to defeat legislation by not reporting it out, what can a favorable House or Senate majority do? There are procedures for extricating a bill from committee, but they are rarely invoked and are even more rarely successful. First, the rules are cumbersome to manipulate, and second, congressional norms work against overriding a committee decision. Consider, for example, a procedure frequently used in the House, the "discharge rule."[26] It provides that a petition to discharge a bill from further committee consideration after thirty days must be signed by a majority of House members. The bill then goes on the Discharge Calendar, and any member who signed the petition may call it for consideration by the House. However, that consideration may take place only on the second or fourth Monday of each month. If the House votes favorably, the bill is considered immediately.

[26] Lewis A. Froman, Jr., *The Congressional Process* (Boston: Little, Brown, 1967), p. 93.

Between 1923 and 1960, members of the House submitted 344 discharge petitions. But only eighteen discharged bills passed the House. And in the forty years, only two became law.[27] A factor not reflected in the statistics is that the discharge rule may force a reluctant committee to act. Once a chairman sees the names on a petition approaching a majority, he may hasten to report the legislation. Following the Supreme Court's 1962 decision on prayer in the public schools, a multitude of bills on the issue descended on the House Judiciary Committee. Liberal Chairman Emanuel Celler kept the legislation in committee until a discharge effort was mounted in 1964 by a bipartisan conservative coalition. The Judiciary Committee reported a bill.[28] But with this qualification understood, the low success rate for discharge petitions underlines one point of congressional practice that may be ignored in charges of committee "obstructionism." Quite simply, bills that cannot pass the committee usually cannot pass on the floor. If political opposition is strong enough to influence the committee, it is likely to be strong at other points in the Congress. At the very least, it is likely to be sufficiently influential to persuade congressmen to adhere to the norms of specialization and reciprocity and not to override the committee's judgment. The past history of federal-aid-to-education bills is a case in point. Bills were submitted from the time of the Truman Administration on, only to be stopped in the House Education Committee under hostile Chairman Graham Barden, Democrat of North Carolina. When Adam Clayton Powell, a proeducation Democrat, became chairman and the committee gained a more liberal membership after 1960, education bills emerged from Education only to be stopped by the Rules Committee, and when they emerged from Rules, they were defeated on the floor. Not until 1965, in the "Great Society" Eighty-ninth Congress, did federal aid to education pass the House floor.

Senate procedures seem simpler on the surface but are equally difficult to operate successfully. The Senate discharge rule is rarely

[27] Malcolm E. Jewell and Samuel C. Patterson, *The Legislative Process in the United States* (New York: Random House, 1966), p. 261.

[28] Froman, *op. cit.*, p. 93.

invoked because it is subjected to four different debatable measures, thus offering the opportunity for four separate filibusters to be waged by the bill's opponents. The most frequently employed method of extrication is addition of committee bills to other legislation as nongermane amendments.[29] The Senate, unlike the House, permits such amendments ("riders") to all but general appropriations bills. The 1960 Civil Rights Act was brought to the Senate floor in this fashion. In introducing an obscure bill on a Missouri school district, Majority Leader Lyndon Johnson announced that it would be open to civil rights amendments. While nongermane amendments are subject to one debatable motion, and thus one threat of filibuster, the relative ease of the process renders it the most practicable procedure.

The cumbersome discharge procedures must be seen in their congressional context. Norms of specialization and committee autonomy prescribe that the committee knows best the business before it. Discharge attempts run counter to the norms and are made in only exceptional circumstances. Moreover, the procedures are sufficiently difficult that only intense and determined majorities can counter committee obstruction. As Lewis Froman concludes:

> The House and the Senate . . . in the way in which they conduct their legislative business are quite different bodies. But the fact that their rules and procedures are quite different should not obscure a major point which they have in common, and that is the possibility for relatively small minorities to delay and defeat legislation which an apathetic majority, if given the opportunity, might approve.[30]

To counter that committee minority, it takes a determined majority and usually the support of the party leadership as well. Discharge procedures are available for those rare occasions when determined majorities can be mobilized.

Committees exert a positive as well as a negative influence. It is the committee's bill that goes to the floor and the committee's judgment that weighs heavily in floor consideration. Committee amend-

[29] *Ibid.*, p. 132.
[30] *Ibid.*, p. 139.

ment may play an important part in getting past the floor: members favorable to legislation will know what their colleagues will or will not accept. Indeed, the White House may find itself told by a chairman that if the President wants some kind of bill, certain amendments will be necessary. Add or delete one clause and the chairman can tell seventeen senators on the floor that their problems are solved.

Wilbur Mills' Ways and Means Committee has been particularly adept at revising Executive Branch measures to secure House passage. In 1958, when the controversial administration proposal to renew the Reciprocal Trade Act came before his committee, Mills announced he would try for a bill the House could accept. He consulted with his colleagues to gear the bill to their sensitivities. He scheduled a months-long series of hearings to provide time to mobilize support. As Mills saw it, "the situation was so unfavorable that it could only improve with time."[31] President Kennedy's tax reform proposal was similarly revised and guided by Mills. In these cases, the committee chairman served as the key liaison point between the executive and the House members.

THE HOUSE COMMITTEE ON RULES

The House Rules Committee is unique in its control over the fate of proposed legislation. House procedure dictates that bills must have rules governing floor debate and amendment. The rules are specified bill by bill—by the Rules Committee. Hence almost all major legislation must survive this stage of the process. The committee's refusal to grant a rule is tantamount to defeat. Private bills and noncontroversial legislation approved by unanimous consent are excepted from Rules consideration. Also excepted are "privileged" measures, such as general appropriations bills, as well as veterans and public works bills (following some obscure congressional logic). For the rest, there are Rules hearings at which the senior members of a bill's substantive committee testify. Rules may negotiate changes in the legislation and/or grant a rule or refuse to grant a rule.

[31] James A. Robinson, *Congress and Foreign Policy-Making* (rev. ed.; Homewood, Ill.: Dorsey, 1967), p. 60.

Rules has a fixed 2 to 1 ratio of majority to minority party members. Both parties have held to regional representation in assignments to the committee. And because of southern dominance in Democratic party membership for several decades, Rules often is controlled by a bipartisan coalition—of conservative southern Democrats and Republicans. Indeed, since the late 1930s, Rules has been notorious as a bottleneck for liberal legislation. In 1961, liberal House Democrats mounted sufficient pressure on Speaker Sam Rayburn to force through an enlargement of the committee from 12 to 15 members, including two additional moderate-to-liberal Democrats. In 1963, the fifteen-member size was made permanent.

Some of its conservative notoriety is deserved. The committee's impact has been largely negative—defeating highly publicized liberal administration bills or delaying legislation to negotiate a more conservative compromise. On the average, the committee considers 150 bills per Congress, denies hearings to about twenty, and denies rules after hearings to approximately twelve more.[32] In the eighty-sixth Congress (that preceding the 1961 "liberalizing"), Rules blocked or delayed action on at least six controversial measures: minimum wage legislation, civil rights, depressed areas legislation, postal pay raise, omnibus housing, and federal aid to education.

However, the predominant pattern is one of cooperation between the committee, the leadership, and the substantive committee chairmen in granting rules. Many of the refusals are at the request of the leadership—a fact not sufficiently appreciated by the casual observer of the congressional scene. The party leadership may ask the committee not to grant a rule for legislation it opposes but fears may command a majority on the floor. Such is alleged to have occurred with the 1964 national fair-trade bill.[33] Or Rules may be asked to delay a bill the leadership supports but fears will not win majority support (as with the 1964 Area Redevelopment Bill). The committee then can save the leadership from embarrassing

[32] James A. Robinson, *The House Rules Committee* (New York and Indianapolis: Bobbs-Merrill, 1963), as cited by Froman, *op. cit.*, pp. 53, 54.
[33] Froman, *op. cit.*, p. 64.

victories and defeats. In view of this role as congressional scape-goat, part of its notoriety may not be deserved. The Committee resists perhaps three or four bills per Congress in clear opposition to the leadership. The predominant pattern is cooperation between the Committee and the leadership, interspersed with occasional, highly publicized conflict.

After a bill has been in Rules for seven days, it may be extricated by a discharge procedure similar to that used for standing committees. Or it may be dislodged by Calendar Wednesday proceedings. Each Wednesday, an alphabetical call of the committee is privileged business whereby a substantive committee may call to House consideration any bill which it has reported, thus bypassing Rules. Calendar Wednesday, like the discharge procedure, is cumbersome to manipulate. A committee may wait weeks for its turn and, once used, must wait for a second turn until all other committees are called. Further, because action on the bill must be completed that day, the opposition is encouraged to talk and maneuver the House into Thursday.

Variations on a much simpler device, the "21-day rule," were tried by two congresses. The rule, passed in 1949, empowered the substantive committee chairman to call up the legislation after it had been held in Rules for 21 days. It was repealed in 1951. The 21-day rule passed in 1965 empowered the Speaker to recognize a member from the standing committee for the purpose of calling up legislation for House consideration. It too did not survive the midterm election. On January 10, 1967, its first business day, the more conservative Ninetieth Congress repealed the 21-day rule. Voting on repeal was as follows.[34]

	For	Against
Northern Democrats	6	141
Southern Democrats	69	18
Republicans	157	26
Total	232	185

[34] *Congressional Quarterly Weekly Report* (January 13, 1967): 398.

The northern Democratic votes that had helped pass the rule after the 1964 Johnson landslide simply were gone from Congress after 1966. The GOP had gained 47 seats.

THE COMMITTEE SYSTEM AND THE DISTRIBUTION OF INFLUENCE

While influence over policy is decentralized by the assignment of areas of jurisdiction to committees, the degree of decentralization varies from committee to committee. As the preceding discussion makes clear, some may be, in effect, "little legislatures" in managing conflict and policy-making. Others may serve merely as points of prior consideration for the House or Senate. One major question of influence concerns the site where decisions are made. When is a bill recommended by a committee amended or defeated on the floor? And when does the committee's decision become the Senate's or House's decision?

A number of factors contributing to a committee's effectiveness can be suggested, derived from the variation in subject matter, membership, and chairmen noted above. (1) The prestige of the committee, reflected in the pecking order of transfers or the seniority of the members, may facilitate floor acceptance of legislation. (2) The cohesiveness of the membership may also facilitate acceptance. Unanimous reports from committees carry more weight than divided committees and especially more than committees where minority reports are filed objecting to provisions in the majority's bill. Accordingly, characteristics contributing to cohesiveness become noteworthy: consensus on goals; the legislative orientation of members directed toward accommodation and compromise; the stability of the membership, found in the prestigious committees, which permits socialization into the committee's goals. (3) The prestige of the chairman and his relationship with the committee's majority may exercise an independent influence. A prestigious chairman, supported by his committee's majority, can add considerable persuasiveness to doubtful legislation on the floor. And (4) the subject matter under consideration may affect outcomes: in particular, whether the subject matter is of interest to congressmen outside the committee; whether it involves controversy; and whether it allows the kind of "split the difference" compromise that can be satisfied at the committee stage.[35]

At one extreme, the House Appropriations Committee's recommendations are virtually always accepted by the House. Informal expectations of House members yield to the committee the effective decision-making on appropriations. Representatives agree that to do otherwise—to open up to the full House the enormous and complex subject of how much and where federal money should be spent— would result in chaos. Further, controversy is minimized by virtue of the nature of money bills. They may be compromised. As Richard Fenno explains it:

> The subject matter keeps Committee members relatively free agents, which promotes intra-Committee maneuvering and, hence, conflict avoidance. Members do not commit themselves to their constituents in terms of precise money amounts, and no dollar sum is sacred—it can always be adjusted without conceding that a principle has been breached.[36]

Moreover, Appropriations members are selected for their ability to compromise and from the chamber's senior "responsible legislators." They share the same goals: the committee should "guard the Treasury" against executive onslaught and reach consensus on policy. Each factor reinforces the other. The importance of subject matter attracts senior representatives to an assignment that increases their prestige. The committee's prestige and solidarity and the nature of the subject matter work together to ensure that Appropriations and its specialized subcommittees will determine policy for the House.

By contrast, the Senate Banking and Currency Committee has been a fairly low prestige assignment, bringing together members with diverse and conflicting points of view—and some with no interest in the subject matter. The committee has had perhaps more than its share of mavericks. For example, in the Eighty-eighth Con-

---

[35] Cf. Fenno's analysis in "The House Appropriations Committee . . ." of the five contributing factors to "integration" presumed to affect the committee's effectiveness on the floor. The five factors are subject matter, consensus, legislative orientation of members, stability of membership, and the committee's attractiveness. I have added—with Manley, "Wilbur Mills . . ."—the independent effect of the chairman.

[36] Fenno, "The House Appropriations Committee . . . ," p. 312.

gress it included Paul Douglas, Joseph Clark, and William Proxmire, plus a Democratic chairman, A. Willis Robertson, who voted consistently with the Republicans and a Republican member, Jacob Javits, who voted consistently with the Democrats. In the early 1960s, besides the more esoteric banking and savings and loan issues, the committee considered such controversial programs as public housing, mass transportation, and legislation for depressed areas. These programs, which were vigorously pushed by liberal Democratic Presidents, split the Congress into liberal and conservative camps and were brought to a committee itself ideologically polarized. The membership included senators who scored highest or lowest in support of the conservative coalition and senators who were most or least in support of a larger federal role. Hearings reflected these divisions. Floor debates frequently became continuing debates between committee members. Even on less controversial issues, conflict erupted. Chairman Robertson's "specialty" was the banking laws, but maverick Proxmire battled the chairman during floor consideration of banking legislation. Douglas periodically aired the committee's disagreements—for example, he complained to the Senate at large that Robertson refused to schedule hearings on his Truth-In-Lending Bill. In addition to the committee's low prestige, the large number of mavericks, and ideological polarization, there was the disruptive influence of the chairman. Robertson, the ideological opposite of his Democratic colleagues on the committee, resembled Proxmire and Douglas in one way: He did not choose to work for committee unity or effectiveness on the floor. It is not surprising, then, to find that in the Eighty-eighth Congress the committee's "decisions" did not automatically become the Senate's decisions. For 1963–1964 the *Congressional Quarterly* records nine committee bills. Three were defeated in committee; two, routine administration bills of little general interest, were recommended by the committee and accepted by the Senate; four were amended on the floor or defeated.[37]

[37] The Eighty-eighth Congress bills include S750, HR9609, S1799 defeated in committee; HR12267, and S1642 passed; and S3049, S298, S1163, and S6 amended or defeated on the floor.

The Senate Foreign Relations Committee presents a different mix of factors. From the Eighty-first through the Eighty-fifth Congresses, its recommendations were accorded a high rate of floor acceptance. Of 213 committee-approved bills and resolutions, 194, or 91 percent, were subsequently passed by the Senate. Seventeen were not acted on, and one, which the committee reported adversely, was defeated. Only 20 percent of its bills were amended on the floor. James Robinson concludes that for foreign relations, the "committee's decision became the Senate's decision."[38] During that span there were four chairmen—including Tom Connally (Texas Democrat), Alexander Wiley (Wisconsin Republican), the highly prestigious Walter George (Georgia Democrat), and Theodore Green (Rhode Island Democrat). Hence, it is difficult to attribute the committee's influence to the chairman's work. However, other factors can be suggested. Foreign Relations is a top prestige committee in the Senate, and for nearly fifty years—after the bitterly fought conflict over membership in the League of Nations and until the Vietnam war became so divisive an issue—the subject itself evoked little clientele interest or Senate controversy. Major foreign policy decisions had become an executive prerogative. Treaties, ambassadorial appointments, and resolutions on foreign policy provided the Senate its opportunity to participate in policy-making, but even these aroused no continuing Senate interest and were considered ad hoc decisions. Thus the Senate traditionally allowed its prestigious committee, whose members were interested in the field, to make decisions for the Senate as a whole.

The House Ways and Means Committee provides an example of a very prestigious and carefully selected membership, charged with extremely controversial legislation. Taxes, trade, social security, the bread-and-butter constituency interests, are of vital concern to all congressmen. They are highly partisan issues as well. Countering this effect, however, is the esoteric nature of the subject matter. All congressmen may be interested in tax policy, but few are able—or want—to work through the intricacies of tax legislation. Ways and

[38] Robinson, *Congress and Foreign Policy-Making*, p. 73.

Means frequently divides on party and/or ideological lines, but, according to John Manley, a norm of "restrained partisanship" pervades its business. Members try to agree. They compromise where they can. Where party solidarity makes compromise impossible, minority reports may be submitted. According to one Republican:

We deal with things on which Republicans and Democrats are in basic, fundamental disagreement and when you have something like this you are bound to get disagreement and minority reports. I think the major reason things don't disintegrate is Mills. . . . Members agree that Mills *acts for* the committee "to ensure its effectiveness on the floor."[39]

And in Mills' view, the committee's reputation is dependent upon House acceptance of its bills. Virtually all major Ways and Means bills are considered under a closed rule, which precludes floor amendments unless they are first accepted by the committee. Further, Mills has the astounding record of being beaten only twice in his years as chairman on a committee-reported bill of any consequence. As noted above, he will not report a bill he believes cannot pass the House. Manley summarizes:

The Committee is widely thought to be the master of its esoteric subject matter and almost every member has a stake in maintaining this reputation. The House expects the Committee to polish its bills to near perfection technically and, perhaps more important, to make a satisfactory adjustment of the competing demands which surround Ways and Means bills.[40]

The importance of a committee's unity in achieving floor acceptance is indirectly attested to by the effort Mills expended to achieve unity. In this case, the legislative orientation of the members, the prestige of the committee, and the political skill of the chairman all have contributed to the Committee's effectiveness in the full House.

Still unexplored is the question of the relative importance of the various contributing factors considered singly and in combination. That question will need to wait for additions to the still-sparse

[39] John Manley, "The House Committee on Ways and Means . . . ," *American Political Science Review*, (December 1965): 932.

[40] *Ibid.*, pp. 927–939, especially p. 931.

literature on committees. The cases above at least serve to demonstrate the variation in committee autonomy and take us one step further than we were. It seems likely that the congressional norm of specialization plus the committee's own efforts to achieve effectiveness work to allow most committees the decisive say on most bills under their jurisdiction. However, some committees achieve no such effectiveness, and under certain conditions others will face floor challenge, amendment, or defeat. The committee system decentralizes influence over policy but allows multiple outcomes and multiple sites for decision. These outcomes are shaped in part by the membership and the chairmen and in part by the nature of the subject matter and the consequent intervention of other participants in the policy-making process. Party leaders, executive and clientele groups, other congressmen—all may extend legislative consideration beyond the committee stage.

CHAPTER 6

PARTY AND PARTY LEADERSHIP

So far, the accent has been on decentralization and dispersion of power. Representational roles, congressional norms of seniority and specialization, the division of labor by committees—each providing some reciprocated support for the other—together serve to distribute power widely. But there is another structure which provides a necessary consolidation of influence. That is the political party. All congressmen share loyalty to one or the other party. They have all been elected to Congress as partisans. (The exceptional independent should not distract attention from this basic fact.) The physical structure of the House and Senate reflects the political. Aisles divide the two parties. Cloakrooms, office space, and softball teams are partisan. Committee membership and seniority are accorded by party lists. All of this points to the fundamental fact of dualism. Congressmen are not only representatives of separate constituencies; they are also Republicans or Democrats.

Party organizes and centralizes congressional action in two ways. First, it structures the members' loyalties. There is some likemindedness of fellow partisans to start with. Add to this the socialization into party loyalty by the past political career. And add to this the influence of the congressional norm of party loyalty. Together these produce coherence of opinion within one party and division between the two. Second, party provides a base for centralized leadership which further consolidates members' loyalties. While congressmen feel more comfortable voting with the party, rather than against it, constituency, conscience, or intracongressional agreements can cause them to defect. The party may be considered a reservoir of support for programs yielding full or very meager results. It is the leaders' job essentially to tap that reservoir to its greatest capacity—to strengthen party cues over other cues which may influence decisions.

The only centralized leadership in Congress is based on party. Speakers, floor leaders, whips, and conference and policy chairmen owe their selection and their continuing support to the members of their congressional party. The Speaker of the House is the one office that extends beyond party lines to the chamber as a whole. But the Speaker actually is the leader of the majority party in the House. At the beginning of a new Congress, each party nominates a candidate for Speaker. But since members of the majority party almost always vote for their party's nominee, as do the members of the minority party for their nominee, the "election" is merely an automatic ratification of the majority party's choice. With the exception of the Speaker, all other formal leadership positions are matched in both parties. There is a Democratic and a Republican floor leader, a Democratic and a Republican whip, and so on. This duplication of posts itself suggests how firmly rooted leadership is in the congressional party organization.

Speakers and floor leaders share party leadership with the President—when their party controls the White House. From this comes a fundamental ambivalence in the congressional leader's role. He is both a Presidential spokesman in Congress and a congressional leader, and at times the two roles may be incompatible. Speaker Joe Martin of Massachusetts complained of his unpopular task of persuading House Republicans to support Eisenhower proposals, which many found "too similar to the Roosevelt and Truman policies they had been accustomed to opposing."[1] But Martin worked for the Eisenhower program even when that meant a long and bitter

[1] Joseph Martin, *My First Fifty Years in Politics* (New York: McGraw-Hill, 1960), p. 229.

fight with his friend and Ways and Means Chairman Reed over the excess profit tax. Senate leader William Knowland of California had even more difficulty reconciling the two roles. Knowland fought for the Bricker amendment, which the President opposed. He left his desk and explained on the floor that he had done so "because . . . what I say is not said as majority leader, but . . . in my capacity as an individual Senator of the United States."[2]

The Knowland case, however, is exceptional. The contemporary expectation seems to be that party leaders will support and will even actively work for Presidential programs. In this way, parties, through the mediation of congressional leaders, serve to coordinate Presidential and legislative support for programs.

Leaders influence followers, but the followers affect the nature of the leadership as well. Congressional membership is collegial, from its fundamentally egalitarian basis in geographical representation. It is partisan, with two parties enjoying different regional and state bases of strength. It is senior and stable, with some variation in party strength occurring from one Congress to the next. (Some 45 to 50 of 435 House seats may regularly shift back and forth between parties; small as it is, this variation has considerable consequences for the congressional parties.) The following discussion attempts to show how these characteristics (1) define the extent and limits of leadership, (2) provide the basis for the selection of leaders and the support they command, and (3) shape, in part, the range and success of party strategies on policy. Parties, in this way, are a central link between patterns of congressional action. They organize and shape policy outcomes, and they are shaped by the underlying distribution of members.

HOUSE PARTY LEADERSHIP

A tracing of the major positions of party leadership can show the House solution to leadership in a collegial context. Quite simply it is this: The formal leaders of the House have limited resources for

---

[2] Randall B. Ripley, *Majority Party Leadership in Congress* (Boston: Little, Brown, 1969), p. 130.

influence, in the rules and the expectations of the members, that the average congressman does not possess.

SPEAKER OF THE HOUSE

The Constitution mandates that "The House of Representatives shall choose their Speaker and other officers," and that "Each house may determine the rules of its proceedings. . . . There has always been a Speaker, but the rules and expectations surrounding his office have changed periodically. While the Speaker was considered leader of his party in the nineteenth-century House, he usually had to share power with ruling cliques or a few key committee chairmen. Consolidation of power under the Speaker came toward the end of the century, between 1896 and 1910, with a series of innovations by Speakers Randall, Carlisle, Reed, Crisp, and Cannon. They strengthened the Speaker's power of recognition; strengthened the Rules Committee as an instrument of the Speaker; engineered the "Reed Rules" which barred the almost traditional dilatory motions and filibustering; and employed power over committee assignments and the appointing and demoting of chairmen. Obviously, each of these innovations could be—and was—used to influence legislation.[3] Institutional and personal rule reached an apex with the Speakership of Joseph Cannon (1903–1910) and was followed by a reaction in 1910. In the revolt of 1910 and 1911, the Speaker was stripped of key power, notably his control over chairmanships and committee assignments and his seat on Rules. But the Speakership was not stripped of all power. Twentieth-century Speakers have not been reduced to the situation of their pre-1890 counterparts.

A second kind of dramatic change in the office concerns the seniority of Speakers and the "professionalization" of House careers. In the nineteenth century, a House seat was considered a "good thing" which should be passed around. The House was characterized by rapid turnover of members, brief service before election as Speaker, and frequent retirement from the post as Speakers turned

[3] *Ibid.*, pp. 49, 87–89.

to pursue other political careers. The classic case is Henry Clay, who was elected Speaker in his first House term. He resigned three years later, in 1814, to accept an appointment as commissioner to negotiate the Treaty of Ghent with Great Britain. He returned *twice* more and was elected Speaker both times. And each time he resigned, once to serve as John Quincy Adams' Secretary of State.

By the turn of the century the influx of newcomers decreased. The average service of nonfreshmen lengthened. With the "professionalization" of the House membership came a professionalization of the Speakership.[4] Speakers tended to compile increasingly greater seniority before their election to the post. Twentieth-century Speakers have had from 15 to 34 years prior service in the House! And they have tended increasingly to hold prior posts of leadership in the congressional party—either as floor leader or committee chairman. And once elected Speaker, they tend to stay in office until death or retirement from public life.

If the modern Speaker's power does not match that wielded by a Joseph Cannon, it still is considerable. He has the power of recognition of speakers on the floor, which gives him considerable control over the course and timing of debate. In doubtful cases, he may decide which committee should receive a bill. With the advice of the parliamentarian, the Speaker rules on the appropriateness of parliamentary procedure. He appoints House members to conference committees, and he has the final responsibility for scheduling legislation. (While scheduling is mainly the job of the floor leader, this is carried on in consultation with the Speaker whose wishes are controlling.) The Speaker also can influence the party's committee on committees in the making of assignments.

Power over assignments is less than at the turn of the century when a Speaker could interfere with the seniority ranking and remove obstreperous committee members and chairmen, elevating others more congenial with his policies. He can no longer interfere

4 Nelson Polsby, "The Institutionalization of the U.S. House of Representatives," *American Political Science Review*, (March 1968): 144–168.

with seniority. But he can influence the appointment of new members and the assignment of members seeking transfers, and so retains some control over the shaping of committee membership. Sam Rayburn, for example, ensured that those appointed to Ways and Means would support reciprocal trade and oppose changes in the oil depletion allowance. At one point Rayburn "liberalized" the Education and Labor Committee by encouraging the appointment of specific junior Democrats.[5]

Perhaps most important is the Speaker's central position in the House communication network. This power in a way is a combination of all power listed above. By the fact that he (1) is the presiding officer, (2) sets the agenda, (3) leads a whip organization charged with gathering information, and (4) knows who wants what committee assignment, the Speaker is at the center of information and communication in the House. In a large and decentralized organization, where information is a highly prized political resource, such a position carries considerable power of its own.

With these resources, the Speaker must attempt to perform a number of functions. He is charged with House maintenance. He must see to it that House business runs smoothly—that disruptive conflicts are avoided. He is also charged with maintenance of the congressional party. He must head off serious conflicts within the party and supervise the floor leaders and whips. If the President is of his party, he must conduct liaison with the White House. And finally, he must mobilize support for party or Presidential programs. This is the crux of party leadership, where the powers outlined above may be needed in full and then supplemented by personal skills. On difficult or controversial bills, the Speaker must enlist the whip organization, scheduling strategies and favors past and future, to mobilize the necessary support at all stages of the legislative process, and yet at the same time keep the House from being convulsed in the conflict.

[5] Randall B. Ripley, *Party Leaders in the House of Representatives* (Washington, D.C.: Brookings Institution, 1967), p. 22.

MAJORITY LEADER

The majority leader did not become a separate House office until 1899.[6] Prior to that time, the chairman of Ways and Means was usually considered majority floor leader. If he could not lead, the Speaker would enlist another member for specific legislation. From 1899 to 1919, the majority leader was also Ways and Means chairman, but the two positions were recognized to be clearly separate, although given to the same man. Since 1919, the two posts have become completely separated. The post assumed major importance under Oscar Underwood (1911–1915) who overshadowed the Speaker, but the most common situation, and the current one, is of subordination to the Speaker. The majority leader is chief lieutenant to the Speaker.

The majority leader's major function is to assist the Speaker in the tasks discussed above. Specifically, he is charged with scheduling legislation. His office is the central point for day-to-day communication concerning the House agenda. He also is responsible for floor leadership. The majority leader conducts most of the procedural debates and a considerable amount of substantive debate, especially on bills of importance to the party. Like the Speaker, he also must try to mobilize support for party proposals. While the majority leader's power is derivative from the Speaker's, his role in scheduling and floor debates and his central position in the House communication network make the job considerably attractive to the ambitious congressman. Further, the growing practice, at least among the Democrats, of recruiting Speakers from the majority leader's post adds to the attractiveness and potential prestige of the office.

MINORITY LEADER

The candidate nominated for Speaker by the minority party—the losing candidate—becomes the minority leader. While he does not have the Speaker's power over recognition, procedure, or agenda

---

[6] George Galloway, *History of the House of Representatives* (New York: Thomas Y. Crowell, 1961), p. 211; Ripley, *Party Leaders in the House*, p. 24.

setting, he still consults with the Speaker on these matters. The Speaker cannot forget that some day the positions may be reversed. The minority leader may influence his party's committee assignments. As head of his party and because of his proximity to the Speaker, the minority leader also occupies—and gains the influence of—a central place in the House communication network. Like the Speaker, the minority leader leads his party in the House. He too is charged with the welfare of the congressional party and he must mobilize support for party strategies. He consults with the majority leader on scheduling, and, like the majority leader, supervises floor leadership. He is also chief spokesman for party positions in the House.

Yet the minority leader's job is quite different from those of his two counterparts in the majority. With less opportunity to enact party policy into law, the minority leader has the special problem of bolstering morale among members that find themselves both less informed about what the House is doing than the majority party members, and on the losing side much of the time in the committee and on the floor. A number of writers have suggested the minority leader may be the target of "frustrations" attributable to minority party status. And it is true that minority party leaders tend to retire more frequently, and to be retired by their congressional party more frequently, than Speakers. Randall Ripley concludes: "Clearly, working in the majority is much more satisfying, and safer, than working in the minority."[7]

WHIP ORGANIZATIONS

Leadership in each party is served by an extensive whip organization. The first House whips were appointed at the turn of the century. By the 1930s, the whips had developed into a large-scale operation, with deputy whips and regional whips serving the chief whip. In general, whips have little independent power. They serve the party leadership by ensuring attendance on the floor and trans-

[7] Ripley, *Majority Party Leadership*, p. 32; see also Charles O. Jones, *The Minority Party in Congress* (Boston: Little-Brown, 1971).

mitting information between the leadership and the party members. This communication includes polling members on important legislation, informing the leaders about sure and doubtful votes, and if necessary, pressuring the wavering or uncommitted. An important and close vote may produce several whip polls and continuing communication with members. It is the whips' responsibility to see that the necessary members are on the floor when votes are to be taken. This involves persuading members not to leave Washington. If they have left, it requires providing for their immediate return— by airplane, helicopter, or wheelchair—or arranging pairs when members must be away. In a body as large as the House, information is a politically crucial commodity. The whips are indispensable lieutenants of the leadership.

THE LIMITS OF LEADERSHIP

The crux of majority leadership in the House is mobilizing sufficient support for party proposals at each stage of the legislative process. It is within this context that the limits of leadership can be seen. One major limiting factor is the existence of other leaders—most notably, the committee chairman. A bill may be stopped or completely rewritten at the committee stage. Or a chairman may not schedule hearings. Party leaders have few sanctions to apply to the recalcitrant chairman, protected as he is by the seniority system. Given this independent and joint control over particular legislation, negotiation and cooperation between the two kinds of leaders are crucial. As Richard Fenno describes it:

Most of the time the two kinds of leaders cooperate—sometimes on the basis of a policy agreement, but always on the basis of a mutual need. The party leaders need the support of the committee leaders if they want any bill at all to get to the floor. The committee leaders need the support of the party leaders if they want procedural assistance and sufficient supporting votes on the floor. So committee leaders remain amenable to the wishes of the party leaders, but the party leaders by and large defer to and support the specialized committees.[8]

[8] Richard Fenno, "The Internal Distribution of Influence: The House," in David B. Truman (ed.), *The Congress and America's Future* (Englewood Cliffs, N.J.: Prentice-Hall, 1965), p. 74.

A second limit on House leadership is the Rules Committee, which has a potentially independent influence on legislative scheduling. A bill obstructed in Rules or held there until the session's last-minute rush may seriously upset the leadership's agenda. Even more seriously, it can threaten the bill itself. Yet it should be noted that a delay in Rules can work for the House leadership—a fact often lost sight of because it is leadership-Rules conflicts that are publicized. For example, the House Democratic leadership in the Eighty-eighth Congress, fearful that a mass transit bill would not pass the House, deliberately delayed floor consideration until they could line up additional votes. (They turned out to be Republican votes.) The delay was effected by asking Rules not to report the bill. When the leadership was ready for the bill, Rules immediately reported it out.[9]

A third limit (discussed at length in the concluding section of the chapter) is the size and cohesiveness of the congressional party membership and the lack of discipline available to the leaders to hold party lines. Leaders may count on a core of loyal partisans on every vote. But in some cases the leadership may employ all the resources at its command and the recalcitrant member—happy on a committee, protected by seniority, able to look to other groups in Congress or at home for his base of support—may have little to fear or gain from such persuasion.

SENATE PARTY LEADERSHIP

Some observers have suggested that Senate party leaders are even weaker than their House counterparts, although there is yet no firm evidence on the point. Certainly, the smaller size of the Senate makes a centralized, complex leadership structure less necessary. Until recently, the two Senate party whips alone managed to keep track of their forty to sixty party charges. But by 1970, both Democrats and Republicans had appointed assistant or regional whips to help in the task. Further, the senator has greater visibility and prestige than a representative, which may increase the collegial and shared

[9] Ripley, *Majority Party Leadership*, p. 42.

nature of senatorial power. Senate Majority Leader Lyndon Johnson gave the following capsule summary of his office:

There is no patronage; no power to discipline; no authority to fire Senators like a President can fire members of his Cabinet. . . . The only real power available to the leader is the power of persuasion.[10]

Yet this "power of persuasion" is essentially all that House leaders have also. While there are some differences between House and Senate, the powers of and constraints on the leaders seem at least roughly similar.

First, it should be made clear that the highest formal leadership posts in the Senate are merely ceremonial. The Vice-President is the President of the Senate, and technically the chief presiding officer, who may cast tie-breaking votes. However, since early in the nineteenth century, Vice-Presidents (and senators as well) have found nothing particularly curious in a President of the Senate who does not so much as appear on the premises for several months at a time. The Senate elects a President pro tempore who presides in the absence of the Vice-President. But this is merely an honorary position—traditionally given to the most senior member of the majority party. Unlike the House where the Speaker presides, the Senate gives the actual job of presiding on a day-to-day basis as a chore to its most junior members.

Effective leadership in the Senate resides in the party positions of majority and minority leaders (the floor leaders) and majority and minority whips. The floor leaders have powers roughly comparable to those of their House counterparts. They have the right to be recognized first in floor debate—and to influence who will be recognized when. They control the scheduling of floor consideration of bills, although this task is formally carried out by the Policy Committee. Like the House leadership, they may influence committee assignments of new members or members seeking transfers and the selection of Senate members of conference committees. They are at the center of the Senate's communication network and thus

10 Interview, U.S. News and World Report (June 7, 1960): 88.

are in a position to know who wants what—an awesome power in the hands of a skilled practitioner such as Lyndon Johnson.

Democratic leaders have access to more potential power than Republican leaders because the Democratic floor leader is also chairman of the Conference (that is, of the whole party), chairman of the Steering Committee (which makes committee assignments), and chairman of the Policy Committee (which is responsible for scheduling). The Republicans fill these posts with four different men. Of the four congressional parties, Senate Republicans are the most decentralized in leadership. Charles Jones characterizes the Senate Republican leadership since 1932 as a case of "collegialism" in contrast to the more centralized pattern under the Democrats. Jones points out that while some Republican senators have stood out in influence—for example, Robert A. Taft of Ohio, H. Styles Bridges of New Hampshire, Everett M. Dirksen of Illinois—no one leader has been dominant.[11]

Like the House leaders, Senate floor leaders are expected to mobilize support for party or Presidential proposals. They oversee scheduling and floor debate, often personally leading the floor debate. They see to the maintenance of the party organization in the Senate. If the President is of their party, they maintain liaison with the White House. Senate leaders, too, must work within the boundaries imposed by the separate and independent cadre of leaders in the committee chairs, a lack of party discipline, and a collegial membership which insists on the deference owed a Senator of the United States. An additional check on Senate leaders is their weaker control over floor procedure. No Rules Committee or party leader can limit a senator's right to talk. The filibuster is simply an extreme expression of this privilege. Most Senate business is conducted by unanimous consent, an agreement possible because otherwise no business would be conducted at all.[12] Accordingly, the floor leader's job of facilitating this agreement, soothing ruffled feelings, and so forth, is crucial to the smooth running of the Senate.

[11] Jones, *The Minority Party in Congress.*
[12] Ralph Huitt, "The Internal Distribution of Influence: The Senate," p. 77.

In such an unstructured situation, leaders vary considerably in style and effectiveness. An important determinant of a majority leader's style is his perception of his role. How active and aggressive does he believe the majority leader should be? Lyndon Johnson and Mike Mansfield presumably would answer the question differently, the latter viewing his job more as that of "facilitator" or "moderator" than as that of active leader in policy-making. How does he perceive his relationship to the President? Conceivably a majority leader could be the "President's man" (although this is frowned on in the Senate), or the Senate's "agent" to the President (Taft), or a representative of each to each (Mansfield).[13]

Another important variable is personal skill. Perhaps the best example of adroit use of resources—and one that offers the only available intensive study of a Senate leader—is provided by the Johnson leadership. Johnson served as Democratic floor leader from 1953 through 1960. According to Ralph Huitt's first-hand account,[14] his skill included a willingness to use the resources of the office for persuasion and a talent for friendship. It was said he talked to every Democratic senator every day. He cultivated a good working relationship with the Republican leadership. He was so able to structure a situation that on any particular issue a member could select a role for himself that would not conflict with the party. Johnson evidently was a master at manipulating issues to his (and his party's) maximum advantage. Huitt notes his knack for finding an "umbrella" man on a controversial issue—that is, an esteemed senator with whom other senators could comfortably vote. Thus Senator George of Georgia could provide the umbrella for southern senators on proposals that otherwise might split the party. Johnson simply went first to George. Southerners then were able to vote with the party and still feel southern in doing so.

Senate and House party leaders have fragmentary but nonetheless observable sources of power, which elevates them to positions of "chiefs among equals." House rules define certain prerogatives, and

[13] *Ibid.*, p. 84.
[14] Huitt, "Democratic Party Leadership in the Senate," *American Political Science Review*, (June 1961): 333–344.

in both chambers this power is based, in part, on the members' expectations and perceptions. In an otherwise decentralized organization, composed of political men extremely sensitive to any gradation of power, even a small number of priorities make a big difference.

LEADERSHIP SELECTION AND SUPPORT

The nature of the congressional party membership can also help explain patterns of leadership selection and support. Speakers, floor leaders, and chief whips (with one exception) are formally elected by the party caucus. Only the House Democratic whip is appointed —by the floor leader in consultation with a Democratic Speaker. Since 1965, the House Republican whip has been directly elected. Before that time, appointments were made by the Republican Committee on Committees acting on the advice of a Republican Speaker or minority leader.

Although formally elective, the actual selection bears all the marks of a much more automatic procedure. Leaders stay in their posts for a number of congresses. New leaders are recruited from apprenticeship posts. Whip leads to floor leader. Floor leader to Speaker. The clearest case of this recruitment has occurred with the House Democrats. Throughout two decades Sam Rayburn held sway as Speaker. He was replaced at his death by Majority Leader McCormack, whose position as floor leader was filled in turn by Carl Albert, the majority whip. Rayburn and McCormack had served together as number "1" and "2" in House Democratic leadership since 1940, becoming minority leader and minority whip in the two Republican-controlled congresses. Albert's claim to the floor leadership was challenged by Representative Richard Bolling—a contest described by Nelson Polsby to illustrate the "inside" and "outside" strategies of influence in the House.[15] But after the heat of the preliminary skirmish, Albert, the incumbent whip, won. While the House Demo-

---

[15] Nelson Polsby, "Two Strategies of Influence: Choosing a Majority Leader, 1962," in Robert Peabody and Nelson Polsby (eds.), *New Perspectives on the House of Representatives* (Skokie, Ill.: Rand McNally, 1963).

crats are most noticeable for this predictable recruitment, both Senate Democrats and Republicans exhibit at least one instance of the same process.

Some understanding of this stability can be gained from Table 6.1 which lists occupants of the top House and Senate leadership posts from 1947 through 1966: Speaker, majority and minority leaders, and whips in the House; majority and minority leaders, and whips in the Senate.

If one takes each of the nine organizations of Congress from the Eighty-first (1949–1950) through the Eighty-ninth (1965–1966) as providing opportunity for 67 of the "exceptions" or "violations" shown in Table 6.1 (not counting appointment of new Whips, but counting reappointment of Whips), one finds that only six of the cases—all occurring in the Republican party—could under the most generous estimate be called violations. The three occasions for Senate Republicans involve promotions over Saltonstall, who held the Whip post, to the post of floor leader. But there is no evidence that Saltonstall, who at the time was approaching retirement, wanted the job as floor leader. One instance for the House Republicans merely involves the "compression" in number of posts caused by a change from majority to minority party. In 1949 and 1955, as the Democrats organized the House, Speaker Martin had to step down to become Minority Leader. So Halleck was temporarily removed as Minority Leader since Arends remained Whip. Since, if the hierarchy assumed here were strictly followed, Halleck, not Arends, would have become Whip, this has been counted as one violation. The only two clear-cut violations are Halleck's election over Martin in 1959 and Ford's election over Halleck in 1965. Both defeats involved minority leaders. No speakers have failed reelection. Even counting all six, however, the frequency (9 percent) of times the stability of the process is deviated from is strikingly low. In other words, the selection of leadership is not a choice to be made with each new Congress. Leaders are recruited and predictably returned, enjoying not complete but considerable security in the process.

After the 1968 election, a group of House Democratic liberals, united behind Morris K. Udall of Arizona, attempted to unseat 77-

TABLE 6.1 Party Leadership Stability, 1947–1966

POSITION IN HIER-ARCHY	CONGRESS									
	80TH (1947–48)	81ST (1949–50)	82ND (1951–52)	83RD (1953–54)	84TH (1955–56)	85TH (1957–58)	86TH (1959–60)	87TH (1961–62)	88TH (1963–64)	89TH (1965–66)
House Democratic Leaders										
1	Rayburn	R	R	R	R	R	R	R	M	M
2	McCormack	M	M	M	M	M	M	M	A	A
3		Priest	P		Albert	A	A	A	Boggs	B
									(No. of violations: 0)	
House Republican Leaders										
1	Martin	M	M	M	M	M	<u>Halleck</u>	H	H	<u>Ford</u>
2	Halleck	<u>Arends</u>	A	H	A	A	A	A	A	A
3	Arends			A						
									(No. of violations: 3)	
Senate Democratic Leaders										
1	Barkley	L	McFarland	J	J	J	J	M	M	M
2	Lucas	Myers	Johnson	Clements	C	Mansfield	M	Humphrey	H	Long
									(No. of violations: 0)	
Senate Republican Leaders										
1	White	W	W	<u>Taft</u>	<u>Knowland</u>	K	K	D	D	D
2	Wherry	Salton-stall	S	S	S	<u>Dirksen</u>	D	K	K	K
									(No. of violations: 3)	

NOTE: An initial indicates that the same man continued in office or upon a vacancy was promoted from the next ranking office (that is, "an apprenticeship post"). Underlining indicates an exception to, or "violation" of, the expected procedure—either (1) when a Congressman was removed from his post or (2) when he retained his post but was not raised to a vacant higher leadership position. A change in incumbents for an office where no underlining is shown indicates that the previous incumbent has left Congress—through death, retirement, or a move to the Vice-Presidency.

year-old John McCormack as Speaker of the House. If successful, it would have been the first time in the twentieth century an incumbent Speaker had been defeated. The Udall challenge, however, failed by the decisive margin of 178 to 58. Even a majority of the liberals supported McCormack. Remarked one of the disappointed Udall Democrats: "I don't think we can change this place."[16]

The exceptions to the rule of stability merit a closer examination at this point. In recent congressional history, two minority leaders—both House Republicans—have been ousted. In the days before the organization of the Eighty-sixth Congress, in December 1958, a group of House Republicans met to organize a revolt against incumbent Minority Leader Joseph Martin. The group was disgruntled about the recent net loss of 47 Republican seats in the House and dissatisfied with Martin's past leadership. His health was failing, and the insurgents wanted a more vigorous GOP spokesman. An informal poll of House Republicans indicated that only former floor leader Charles Halleck would command sufficiently widespread support. After being assured that the White House would remain neutral, Halleck announced his candidacy. His backers won the preliminary skirmish over a secret ballot, and Halleck edged Martin, 74 to 71.[17]

The Halleck leadership was to last only six years. After the 1964 election, the process was repeated, this time with Halleck on the receiving end. The dissidents agreed that Gerald R. Ford, Jr., was the best choice around which to rally a revolt. Ford announced his candidacy in December. The two campaigned among House Republicans, although it was observed that Ford campaigned harder. And on the opening day of the Eighty-ninth Congress, he defeated Halleck by secret ballot, 73 to 67.[18] One side note should be added: The Ford forces did not have sufficient "carrying power" to oust Leslie

[16] New York Times, January 3, 1969. The representative was Benjamin Rosenthal of Queens.

[17] Robert L. Peabody, "Party Leadership Change in the United States House of Representatives," American Political Science Review, (September 1967): 685.

[18] Ibid., p. 686. See also Peabody, "The Ford-Halleck Minority Leadership Contest, 1965," Eagleton Institute Cases in Practical Politics, no. 40. (New York: the Institute, 1966).

Arends, who had served twenty years as party whip. Their candidate, Peter H. B. Frelinghuysen of New Jersey, lost to Arends, 70 to 59. Ford could not even get New York's Charles Goodell, one of his major supporters, a seat on the Ways and Means Committee. The Republican Committee on Committees remained in the control of the old guard.

These represent the only two cases of successful challenge in recent House history. No Democrats and no Speakers or majority leaders have been defeated. In the Senate, the only recent instances of effective challenge are Edward Kennedy's 1969 defeat of Russell Long, four-year occupant of the post of Senate Democratic whip, and Kennedy's defeat two years later by Robert C. Byrd of West Virginia.

We can only speculate about, not explain, these exceptions. The House upsets occurred after severe election defeats. In 1958, the Republicans lost 47 seats, and in 1964, the year of the Johnson landslide, they lost 48 seats. But the Kennedy election followed no net change in Senate Democratic strength, although a Democratic Presidential election defeat. And the Byrd victory followed a very minor loss for the Democrats. Yet other years and other election defeats have brought no such overturns. Robert Peabody suggests that election defeat poses "a necessary, but not sufficient, cause of . . . revolt." Defeat creates "a psychological climate within which revolt [can] flourish."[19] Another cause may be the "frustrations" of extended minority party status. This can explain House Republicans but not the absence of cases among Senate Republicans. Presumably, Senate Republicans should have felt as frustrated as House Republicans. Other factors may be the age and skill of incumbents and the proposition of senior to junior members.[20] Peabody suggests that the "pool of senior Democrats" in the House, in contrast to the more junior Republicans, who have been periodically ravaged by election defeat, can help explain the development of hierarchical patterns of succession among House Democrats.

[19] Peabody, "Party Leadership Change . . . ," pp. 686–688.
[20] Ibid., pp. 686–689.

Perhaps the best answer at this point is that it requires an exceptional combination of circumstances to produce such exceptional results. Perceptions of severe electoral defeat, frustrations of extended minority party status, absence of a pool of senior members to support established leadership—all may combine to create conditions under which overthrow could, but not necessarily will, occur. There is a strong indication, then, that congressional elections in the immediate and in the more remote past—which set the structure of membership—help shape the conditions for leadership stability and change.[21]

One kind of change deserves to be noted: the interparty change when the minority party becomes the new majority. Because minority leadership positions are fairly stable, interparty change does not occasion drastic disruption in congressional routine. In the House, the former minority party leader now has the votes to be elected Speaker. The Speaker becomes minority leader. In the Senate the two floor leaders exchange majority and minority roles and responsibilities. The predictability of this exchange has important implications for the conduct of legislative business. The normal pattern is for majority party leaders to consult with minority colleagues on scheduling, committee ratios, and other procedural matters—since one day they will be in the minority, too, and would like the same consideration.

In general, then, change in leaders, even after change in party control, is a smooth and nondisruptive process. Perhaps the smoothest, most friendly transfer of power in the House (possibly the smoothest in any political assembly) occurred at the organization of the Eightieth Congress in January 1947. Partisan lines were sharp and clear. The Republicans had won control of the House for the first time in twenty years and had to come to Congress ready to do partisan battle with a view toward the next Presidential election. Yet, despite the sharpness of the party lines and the keenness of the Democratic defeat, the change of party control in the House from

---

[21] See also my analysis in "Congressional Leadership Selection and Support," *Journal of Politics*, (May 1970): pp. 268–287.

Sam Rayburn to the new Speaker Joe Martin was one of warmth
and friendship. As one observer described it: "Mr. Sam took his
friend Joe by the arm and marched him to the rostrum. He grabbed
the gavel and banged it, much to the delight of both sides of the
aisle, everyone applauding and laughing. . . . " Rayburn and Martin
then exchanged compliments at length.[22]

In this spirit, power passed from Democrats to Republicans in the
Eightieth Congress. Two years later Speaker Martin returned the
gavel to his friend.

PARTY AND COMMITTEE LEADERS

Party leaders can be compared with the "other" leaders of Congress—the chairmen and ranking minority members of the standing
committees. An earlier chapter has treated the committee leaders
and their basis of power in the committees and in the seniority
system. This chapter makes clear that they pose one major limit on
the power of party leaders. But the relation between the two groups
should be described in more detail. What is the degree of overlap
between them? In what ways and on what dimensions are they similar to each other? In what ways are they different?

Perennial pleas are voiced for reform of the seniority system and
a veto over the appointment of chairmen to be exercised by party
leaders. Representative Bolling argues that a Speaker or Senate
Majority Leader's "ability to veto or to replace a [chairman] completely out of step with his party viewpoint . . . would give pause
to the Member who would bolt his party's program."[23] Chairmen
would be kept to the party line by the threat of removal should they
stray too far. If the leadership wanted a Civil Rights bill, Howard
Smith would be in the House scheduling hearings and not home in
Virginia inspecting his barn. The argument has a certain appeal,
but it rests on two critical assumptions. First, it assumes a key difference in outlook between the two kinds of leaders. And second, it

[22] C. Dwight Dorough, *Mr. Sam* (New York: Random House, 1962), pp.
390, 391.
[23] Richard Bolling, *House Out of Order* (New York: Dutton, 1965), p. 241.

assumes that party leaders would be willing to violate the norm of seniority to exercise their veto. Yet, if the norm of seniority governs the selection of both kinds of leaders and produces two groups who have "grown up together" in Congress, party leaders may be no less sensitive to the claim of seniority than their colleagues in the committee chairs that the proposal seeks to discipline. They might also prefer not to punish the man they have had lunch with for the past thirty years. To test the validity of these assumptions, some basic points of similarity and difference must first be established.

CAREER PATTERNS

Although formally elective, the selection of party leaders was seen to exhibit remarkable stability over time and some indication of apprenticeship posts leading to higher posts. Once in office, a party leader is rarely removed. He enjoys security and the expectation that he can advance when a higher post is vacant. This pattern is close to that of the seniority system for selecting chairmen. Once in office a chairman is rarely removed. Committee members "move up" the committee ladder as vacancies occur.[24] Of course, there are fewer "steps" in the apprentice stage for party leaders. The succession is either whip-majority leader-speaker or whip-floor leader.

As might be expected, the groups are similar in terms of congressional seniority. (See Table 6.2.) Both groups are quite clearly congressional seniors—their average age is in the sixties. Both groups have compiled a substantial number of years' service before gaining their leadership posts. Indeed, party leaders outrank committee leaders in congressional seniority in three of the four congressional parties. It is commonly recognized that the seniority rule makes long congressional service a prerequisite for chairmen. But the same apparently is true for party leaders. In 1961, for example, the Speaker of the House (Rayburn) was also the most senior man in the House. The majority leader (McCormack) ranked seventh in congressional seniority.

---

[24] Cf. Fenno's discussion of "seniority-protege-apprenticeship" norms in the House, *op. cit.*, p. 70.

TABLE 6.2 Comparison of Seniority of Party Leaders and Committee
Leaders: 1947–1966

	MEDIAN AGE OF LEADER-SHIP (DURING TERMS OF SERVICE)		MEDIAN NO. YEARS TO GAIN LEADERSHIP		MEDIAN NO. YEARS IN LEADERSHIP POSITION	
	PARTY LEADERS	CC[a] RMM[b]	PARTY LEADERS	CC RMM	PARTY LEADERS	CC RMM
Democrats						
Senate	60	66.0	10	10	6	8
House	62	65.5	21	16	16	6
Republicans						
Senate	64	63.5	11.5	7	3	4
House	62	62.5	16	12	8	6

[a] CC: committee chairmen.
[b] RMM: ranking minority members.

Given this similarly in congressional seniority, it might be expected that party leaders could have succeeded to committee chairs also. To some extent this is the case. Eleven who subsequently became party leaders received committee assignments during the 1947–1966 period. By the time of their elevation to party leadership, four were chairmen or ranking minority members and one held a second rank and three a third rank on committees. There is one clear difference, however, between the two groups: the party leaders' tendency to change committees more frequently than the congressional average and thus lose the committee seniority necessary to gain a chairmanship. This probably explains why even more party leaders had not attained top committee rank.[25]

In sum, the two selection systems seem to be drawing from the same senior stratum of congressional membership. Career patterns are similar in length of prior service, existence of apprenticeship posts, the security that comes from the stability of the process of selection, and in a common dependence on the seniority norm.

On the always touchy question of regional representation in Con-

[25] For a more detailed discussion, see Hinckley, "Congressional Leadership Selection and Support."

TABLE 6.3 Regional Distribution of Members, Committee Leaders, and Party Leaders: 1947–1966

	MEMBERSHIP		COMMITTEE LEADERSHIP		PARTY LEADERSHIP	
	N^a	Predom. Region	N	Predom. Region	N	Predom. Region
				1947–1956		
SD	117	South (52%)	40	South (48%)	6	South (3)
HD	1131	South (51%)	95	South (60%)	4	South (3)
SR	117	None (Midwest 44%; East, 34%)	39	None (Midwest, 49%; East, 41%)	5	None East, (2); Midwest, (2)
HR	1037	Midwest (54%)	95	Midwest (62%)	3	Midwest (2)
				1957–1966		
SD	143	None	40	South (57%)	4	South (2)
HD	1324	None	99	South (62%)	4	South (3)
SR	99	None	37	(East, 46%; Midwest, 35%)	3	West (2)
HR	839	None (Midwest, 43%; East, 36%)	95	Midwest (51%)	4	Midwest (3)

^{a} N = number of congressmen counted for each election won.

gress, further similarities are apparent. Dividing the nation in four regions—East, South, Midwest and West—one can name for each congressional party through a certain span of years the "predominant" regional faction for the full membership, for the committee leaders, and for the party leaders. (A "predominant" faction is here defined as a group comprising more than 50 percent of the members or more than 45 percent with the next largest grouping more than 10 percentage points below.) And one can identify cases where no predominant faction exists. Table 6.3 sets forth the patterns for two decades—1947 through 1956, and 1957 through 1966. In every case except the 1957–1966 Senate Republicans, regional patterns are the same for party and committee leaders. In a number of cases they reflect the same predominance found for the full congressional party membership as well. Where no predominant faction can be identified for congressional party members, the leadership appears to reflect the earlier predominance in members. Thus while the South was losing its predominance in Democratic Party membership in House and Senate that it had enjoyed in the 1947–1956 span, it was still strongly represented in both the committee and party leadership in the following decade. This may be another instance of the "time lag" built into congressional processes.

Policy questions, however, show some differences. Classifying congressmen as liberals, moderates, and conservatives on the basis of their opposition to the Conservative coalition on roll call votes,[26] one finds the results set forth in Table 6.4. Committee leaders are predominately conservative. Party leaders tend to be moderates. The conservatism of chairmen has been discussed in an earlier chapter. However, the "moderateness" of party leaders merits attention here, for it suggests two influences at work on their selection. First, party leaders may be selected from the moderate ranks in order to perform the necessary task of mediating between factions in the party, should such factions exist.[27] Second, since they must not only support, but actively lead their party in Congress, it would seem at minimum that

26 Ibid.
27 Truman, The Congressional Party, pp. 131, 132.

TABLE 6.4 Members, Committee Leaders, and Party Leaders: 1959–1966[a]

		MEMBERSHIP N Predom. Faction		COMMITTEE LEADERSHIP N Predom. Faction		PARTY LEADERSHIP N Predom. Faction
SD	210	None (Moderate, 43%; Conservative, 31%)	62	Conservative (63%)	8	Moderate (7)
HD	918	None (Liberal, 42%; Moderate, 31%)	77	Conservative (57%)	7	Moderate (5)
SR	112	Conservative (80%)	57	Conservative (84%)	8	None (Conservative, 4; Moderate, 4)
HR	567	Conservative (81%)	75	Conservative (83%)	8	Conservative (8)

[a] Numbers refer to congressmen's scores for each congress counted separately. Essentially the same results would be obtained by averaging a congressman's scores. Thus party leaders' average scores yield the following results and the same factional divisions as reported in the table: Senate Democrats, 4 moderates of 4; House Democrats, 3 moderates of 3; Senate Republicans, 1 conservative and 1 moderate of 2; and House Republicans, 3 conservatives of 3.

Scores for party and committee leaders are counted only for congresses when they occupied a leadership post. Since the Speaker does not vote, only scores for floor leaders and whips are included in the House congressional parties.

party mavericks would not be selected. This may not directly explain the moderateness, but it does explain why Democratic conservatives and Republican liberals could not be selected, and why a moderate would be better qualified to communicate with that maverick group than someone further removed on the ideological spectrum.

Despite different ideological tendencies, numerous cases of policy agreement and/or compromise between party and committee leaders can be cited. Of particular interest are cases that touch their common seniority in and loyalty to the congressional institution. For one example, consider Majority Leader Mike McCormack's uncontested election to Speaker, referred to earlier. McCormack was unpopular with both the liberal Democratic Study Group and some southern members. Yet, according to Peabody, McCormack was given strong support by two powerful House chairmen—Carl Vinson and Howard Smith.[28] A second example is Speaker Rayburn's compromise on the Rules Committee issue. Rayburn refused to back the liberal proposal to "punish" William Colmer, second-ranking Democrat on the committee, and other conservatives who had refused to back Kennedy in the 1960 election by stripping them of their seniority and committee posts. After repeated consultation between Rayburn and Rules Chairman Smith—with messengers described as "shuttling back and forth" between them—Rayburn agreed to the Rules Committee enlargement.[29] Liberal Democrat Joseph Clark commented on the decision not to remove Colmer:

That would have constituted a crime against the Establishment, which places far more emphasis on the prerogatives and traditions of the Congress as an institution than it does on a Presidential program. To remove Colmer could have meant tampering with seniority . . . risking a rupture with the Southern wing of the Party.[30]

Rayburn's decision can be seen as a compromise which completely satisfied neither liberal nor conservative faction, but which, given the alternatives, was not wholly unsatisfactory to either. It was, further, a decision taken after consultation with key chairmen and an excellent example of a senior party leader's support of the principle of seniority.

Seen in this light, reformers who propose that the disciplining of chairmen be returned to the party leader's hands (assuming the proposal could ever be accepted in the first place) might be disappointed with the results. Acts that weaken seniority react against the party leaders as well. Besides, committee and party leaders have lived together long enough in Congress to have developed habits of accommodation which facilitate their respective tasks. And finally, both leadership groups are based in a safe, senior congressional

[28] Peabody, "Party Leadership Change . . . ," p. 682.
[29] Bolling, op. cit., p. 216.
[30] Joseph Clark, Congress: The Sapless Branch (rev. ed.; New York: Harper & Row, 1964).

membership to whom they owe -as long as they "keep in touch"—
their continuing support.

ELECTION RESULTS AND PARTY STRATEGIES

"A leader is not free to be any kind of leader he pleases. His
alternatives are framed for him, by the situation." Ralph Huitt goes
on to list some important elements of the "situation." The mood of
the country is one. The activity and aggressiveness of the President
in support of certain legislation is another. A third, the strength of
the party in House and Senate, will be discussed at some length, for
it suggests an important and often overlooked point.[31] Congressional
elections make a difference. Collectively, they define the strength
and factional makeup of the congressional party and, in so doing,
shape the kinds of strategies party leaders can pursue.

To take an obvious illustration, majority leaders can more easily
mobilize support with a large majority (as the Democrats did in the
Eighty-ninth Congress) than with, say, the narrower Democratic
margins in the Eighty-eighth or Ninetieth. In the Eighty-ninth Congress, Democratic House leaders could lose fifty to seventy Democrats on a vote, and no one would even notice. Where narrow
margins divide the parties, leaders may need to bargain, compromise, and count constantly for every vote they can find. The
party's factional makeup is also crucial. With the Democratic Party
split along southern conservative and northern liberal lines, on a
number of issues the Democratic paper "majority" dissolved. In
such cases the term "majority leader" may be misleading. In congresses with narrow party margins and divisions in the ranks, leaders
are trying to build a majority coalition around their minority base of
loyal partisans. In this regard, Randall Ripley differentiates between
"Presidential-partisan" and "Presidential-bipartisan" situations faced
by majority party leaders. Both involve Presidents actively pursuing
a legislative program, but in the former the program can be sup-

---

[31] Huitt, "The Internal Distribution of Influence: The Senate" pp. 82, 83.
Other writers also stress these three variables. See Ripley, *Majority Party
Leadership,* and Jones, *The Minority Party in Congress.*

ported mainly within party ranks. In the latter, the President and congressional leadership must seek bipartisan support, frequently because there are not enough firm partisans to ensure a majority. On most issues (excluding some foreign policy issues where near-unanimous votes are sought), the leadership will stay within the party when they can and look to the minority only when they have to, and then usually at the cost of considerable negotiation and amendments.

To illustrate some of the techniques of the majority party leadership in a Presidential-bipartisan situation, two cases from the Eighty-eighth Congress can be cited. Democrats enjoyed a comfortable, but not overwhelming margin: in the Senate, 67 to 33; in the House, 257 to 178. However, this was a nominal majority because on some issues the southern wing would vote with the Republicans. Leaders in both House and Senate, then, had to ensure *either* sufficient southern Democratic support or Republican support to pass legislation. In 1964, the North Carolina House delegation reacted strongly and adversely to the news that Adam Yarmolinsky was scheduled to play some major role in the poverty program. The full delegation met with the Speaker, demanded a White House promise that Yarmolinsky would not be involved, and threatened that otherwise no North Carolina Democrat would vote for the bill. Chairman Adam Clayton Powell of Education and Labor, the committee handling the bill, and floor manager Landrum were contacted and agreed. The Speaker and Sargent Shriver called the White House and got the required guarantee, and the full North Carolina delegation heard Shriver repeat the promise.[32]

When the South could not be counted on, House and Senate leaders had to look to the Republicans. The most dramatic example is the prolonged consultation between Democratic and Republican Senate leaders on the 1964 Civil Rights bill. Senate Democratic Whip Humphrey consulted with Everett Dirksen, the Republican minority leader almost daily, urging him to discuss his amendments

[32] Ripley, *Majority Party Leadership*, pp. 44, 45, quotes Elizabeth Brenner Drew, "The Politics of Cloture," *Reporter*, (July 16, 1964): 19–23.

with administration leaders. Without Dirksen's—and Republican—support, the administration could not hope to end the southern filibuster and achieve the bill's passage.

The composition of the Congress also shapes the minority party's strategies. Thus Charles Jones distinguishes between "restricted" and "flexible" minorities. The range of strategies available to a minority may be influenced by the size and factional structure of both minority and majority parties. If the majority party needs help, the minority may be in a strong position to bargain for amendments or other concessions—or threaten to try to defeat the program. For example, in the Eighty-seventh Congress, Republican leaders could choose among a number of strategies at the committee stage or on the floor. They could try to defeat legislative proposals repugnant to enough conservative Democrats—as happened with the 1961 Federal Aid to Education bill and the first farm bill of 1962. Or they could try "constructive opposition," where the goal is not defeat, but amendment. Using this strategy, the Republicans failed narrowly on the Omnibus Housing Act and tax reform, but succeeded in the House on the 1961 Minimum Wage bill.[33] Jones contrasts this "flexible minority" with the "restricted minorities" of the Sixty-third and Seventy-third congresses (1913–1914 and 1933–1934). In each, the majority party had an overwhelming numerical advantage, and in the Sixty-third the minority party was badly divided. Under such circumstances there is considerably less the minority leadership can try to do.

This is not to say that the size and structuring of the congressional party are the only influences worth attention. Presidential activity, the country's mood of crisis or complacency, and the style of particular leaders are also important. Certainly, Presidential elections make a difference. For both majority and minority party leaders it makes a crucial difference whether their party controls the White House.[34] And, as was discussed earlier, the pulling power of the Presidential

[33] Charles O. Jones, "The Minority Party and Policy-Making in the House of Representatives," *American Political Science Review*, (June 1968): 492.

[34] See Huitt, "Democratic Party Leadership . . . ," Ripley, *Majority Party Leadership*, and Jones, "The Minority Party and Policy-Making . . . ," p. 482.

coattails may influence a party's strength in Congress. But the size and structure of the party, set collectively by past and present congressional election returns, are in a very real sense parameters of power that set the bounds of strategies available to the congressional party and the limits for what leaders can do.

CHAPTER 7

CONGRESS AND FOREIGN POLICY

Studies of congressional membership and structure would have little relevance if two facts could not be demonstrated. First, that contrary to some popular opinion, Congress plays a major role in national policy-making—both in foreign and domestic spheres. And second, that the major decisions it makes can be understood largely in terms of the key congressional attributes previously discussed: the members' constituency, party, and ideological alignments; their seniority and distribution by committees; the roles of party and committee leaders. This is a large task, made even more difficult by the scarcity of good policy analysis. Very few studies combine a good grasp of both the congressional and the policy spheres. The following two chapters, it should be clear at the outset, are severely limited by the literature on the subject. Nevertheless, the studies which are available do provide some preliminary demonstration.

While political commentaries stress the executive "dominance" of twentieth-century government, it might be appropriate to reaffirm the shared nature of the governing mandate. Major personnel decisions (Supreme Court appointments and ambassadors, for example), financing, and new legislation must be countersigned by both executive and legislative partners. Presidents initiate new executive programs, but Congress supplies the funding. Congress appropriates money, but the President may impound the funds. It is a commonplace to observe that the President has become the twentieth-century

Chief Legislator. But with the proliferation of the federal bureaucracy far beyond the scope of a single executive's sight, in some areas a congressional committee has become the Chief Executive. In the twentieth century Congress has come to look to the executive for legislative initiative. But a congressman will lobby to get a pet project included in a Presidential program. And once introduced by a senator or representative, that executive-sponsored legislation must (1) survive the committee stage, (2) evoke majority support on the floor, (3) be able to duplicate the process in the second chamber, and (4) in case of a difference between Senate and House bills, survive the conference committee and be accepted again by both chambers. All this must be accomplished before that Congress adjourns; leftover legislation must be resubmitted, from the beginning, at the next Congress. If a bill survives this obstacle course, it goes to the President. If the President vetoes it, two-thirds majorities in both houses are required to override the veto. If he signs the bill, it becomes a new public law. Some legislation requires "extraordinary majorities"—two-thirds of the Senate for a treaty, two-thirds of both houses for a constitutional amendment—but otherwise is subjected to the same process as ordinary legislation. Needless to say, through the sequence of discrete attempts to mobilize sufficient congressional support, a Presidential bill may undergo unrecognizable transformation.

Further transformation may occur in the process of executive implementation. If the President may not recognize "his" bill when it emerges from the Congress, the Congress may not recognize its legislation as it is "interpreted" by an executive agency. And the sharing of governing responsibility does not necessarily end even at the stage of implementation. Through the power of congressional oversight, committees may subject once-passed programs to careful scrutiny and review. They may call members of the administration and other witnesses to discover what has been done, how, and to what effect. Congress can discontinue or cut the funds of programs it is dissatisfied with, and so the possibility of future oversight can influence the kind of executive implementation a program receives. "Policy-making," then, is a process of serial interactions between executives, legislators, and other participants. Power is shared, blurred. It shifts and shifts back again in a game that is never over.

Even in foreign policy, traditionally held to be a predominantly executive domain, this same sharing and shifting of power occurs. As Commander-in-Chief, the President oversees the conduct of wars and other military ventures. As Chief of State, he is responsible for the nation's diplomacy. Presidential initiative in this century during America's growing internationalism and cold-war experiments have strengthened the expectation—shared by the public, the congressmen, and other participants—that foreign policy is predominantly an executive responsibility. And yet, constitutionally, Congress declares war and raises armies. The Senate advises on and consents to treaties. The House initiates appropriations for defense and foreign aid. Trade agreements must be legislated. Congressional committees investigate the conduct of a war. And these are not empty formal powers. They have been used on a number of occasions in this century with considerable impact. Congress, responding to strong public sentiment, vetoed President Wilson's League of Nations, held President Roosevelt to European neutrality in the 1930s, and expressed growing dissatisfaction with Presidents Johnson and Nixon in their handling of the Vietnam War.

Moreover, national policy is not distinctively "foreign" or "domestic" in impact. Import quotas, defense projects and trade agreements have both foreign and domestic implications. Even if an individual congressman were willing to grant Presidential responsibility for "foreign policy," he might fight hard for the missile system or sugar quota that would benefit his state or district and view this not as foreign policy-making but as constituency representation. This blurring of policy implications increases the likelihood that foreign policy will be some combined product of executive and legislative endeavor.

This chapter examines the role of Congress in the areas of war and peace, defense policy, and foreign aid. While by no means comprehensive, the discussion can demonstrate the scope and the variation in congressional influence—which extends through all three areas, but with different degrees of persistence and decisiveness. And within those areas of relatively greater influence, the chapter can document the importance of congressional membership and organization on the American foreign policy that results.

WAR AND PEACE

Presidential dominance is clearest in decisions of war or other major military involvement. When Presidents have gone before the Congress to ask for declarations of war or mobilization of men and arms, they have received what they asked for—with speed, little debate, and virtual unanimity. What held for formal declarations of war holds for the recent "nonwars" as well. Presidential declarations of military emergency have produced immediate congressional support, even when details cannot be provided and the scope of subsequent necessary action remains undefined. This was the case with the 1964 Tonkin Gulf Resolution, which initiated the wider American involvement in Vietnam. [The Tonkin Gulf Resolution has since been repealed (twice).] Another such case occurred with the Formosan Resolution of 1955. When in September 1954, the Peiping government attacked Quemoy and reaffirmed their resolution to "liberate" Taiwan, the Eisenhower administration sought a congressional joint resolution authorizing the President to use military force to protect Formosa. Senator Walter George, Chairman of the Foreign Relations Committee and highly prestigious Senator from Georgia, was consulted in advance and approved. Other congressional leaders were briefed. Some members privately expressed misgivings, but the joint resolution was passed 410 to 3 and 85 to 3.[1]

Further, when recent Presidents have reported on *prior* actions taken or decided without specific congressional authorization, they have received support for what has already been done. The Korean decision of 1950 is a case in point. After President Truman had reached his decision to commit United States troops to South Korea, he discussed the decision with some congressional leaders. These

[1] James Robinson, *Congress and Foreign Policy-Making* (rev. ed.; Homewood, Ill.: Dorsey, 1967), pp. 54, 55.

included Senate and House party leaders and some senior members of the Foreign Relations, Foreign Affairs, and Armed Services committees—fourteen congressmen in all. Evidently Chairmen Tom Connally and John Kee of the Senate and House foreign policy committees suggested revisions in the language of the United Nations resolution which the United States was about to propose. But formally the Congress was not asked for its advice or consent. Even the congressional leaders were given only a pro forma briefing and told the decision at the same time as the press. The other members of Congress read about it in the newspapers.[2] For a second case, in the Cuban missile crisis Kennedy's decision on the embargo was arrived at after a week of consultation within the Executive and White House staff, with no congressional representatives present. The decision was made, a speech drafted. On Sunday, the British Ambassador, O'Brien, and Salinger were informed and O'Brien was told to round up a number of congressional leaders for a White House briefing. On Monday, Kennedy held conferences, met with the congressional leaders at 5:00 P.M. and at 7:00 addressed the nation.[3] (Some congressmen reacted to the picture briefing in the same way a number of the earlier consultants had reacted, and thought the blockade irrelevant and indecisively slow. Charles Halleck announced he would support the President, but wanted the record to show that he had been informed at the last minute, not consulted.)[4] For a third case, in the earlier Cuban decision on the Bay of Pigs, the only congressman consulted before the event was Fulbright, Chairman of the Senate Foreign Relations Committee, who incidentally was reported to be the only one who strenuously objected to the plan.

One exception to the pattern traced above occurred during the first Eisenhower administration. With the French losing Indochina in the spring of 1954, President Eisenhower prepared to use United States air and naval forces to support the French. He asked the

2 *Ibid.*, p. 50.
3 Theodore Sorensen, *Kennedy* (New York: Harper & Row, 1965), pp. 672–703.
4 *Ibid.*, p. 702.

Secretary of State to consult with congressional leaders for a joint resolution to that effect. Dulles, the Chairman of the Joint Chiefs, and other executive officials called in some selected congressmen to explain the need for the resolution. Included were Republican and Democratic party leaders and Senator Russell, ranking Democrat on the Senate Armed Services Committee. Dulles argued the imminent fall of the French forces in Indochina (and subsequent fall to Communism of the rest of Southeast Asia) if American help were not immediately provided. Congressional questioning revealed that the other Joints Chiefs did not support the idea and that American allies had not been consulted. The meeting ended without congressional support even from the Republicans present and no further administration action was taken at the time. Chalmers Roberts of the *Washington Post* called it "The Day We Didn't Go to War,"[5] and the withholding of congressional support was clearly instrumental in that decision.

That case, however, remained the exception to the normal coldwar pattern—maintained until the late 1960s—of Presidential decision and congressional assent. Possibly the lack of Presidential decisiveness made the difference. One wonders whether Presidents Kennedy and Johnson would have made a similar response—and whether congressmen would have been consulted at all. Or possibly the opportunity for questioning from congressmen playing the role of "outside critic" made the difference. No such opportunity was provided preceding the Bay of Pigs decision. In any case, whatever else the separation of powers may do or not do, it seems clear it has not kept Presidents from taking decisive military action when that action was deemed necessary by Presidential definition. On such occasions, the congressional "role" has been to supply—along with the rest of the nation—positive support for the President.

Serious questions, however, remain as to whether such docility is an appropriate role or whether more extensive congressional questioning and consultation should be demanded. It is certainly not

[5] Chalmers Roberts, "The Day We Didn't Go To War," *The Reporter* (September 14, 1954): 31–35.

enough to say that "secrecy" or "the need for immediate action" make congressional consultation impossible. Few of the decisions discussed above required immediate action. All of them, even the Cuban missile crisis, allowed the Presidents to select some consultants. While no one maintains there should be a full-dress congressional debate on the subject, some senior, "specialized" committee chairmen and ranking members might well claim they should be among those consulted.

One thing seems clear. If Congress is to play a larger role in such decisions, the demand must come from the congressmen and, ultimately, from the public. Dissatisfaction with the war in Vietnam has brought increased congressional activity—especially from the prestigious Senate Foreign Relations Committee under Chairman and Vietnam critic Fulbright. Nixon's move on Cambodia in the Spring of 1970, without congressional consultation and in the face of known opposition, raised the issue in its sharpest form. The resulting Senate uproar forced a White House briefing for key Senate and House committees and Presidential conciliation on troop withdrawals. Buttressed by widespread public opposition to the war, the Senate undertook legislation restricting funds for American involvement in the war and setting a timetable for withdrawal. The event is too recent to be seen in the larger perspective, but that Senate reaction may help define for future Presidents at least the outer limit of congressional acquiescence.

Further observations can be made from the Senate debate in the spring and summer of 1970. First, the Senate became more than normally active in the making of "war policy" when public opinion became aroused. And second, with increased Senate criticism of the President's handling of the war, the political parties emerged as the main structure through which Senate debate took place. With a Republican President in the White House, Democrats in Congress could give clearer voice to their "dovish" inclinations than they could in the previous Democratic administration. Antiwar voting in the Ninety-first (Nixon) Congress showed clear party lines, with more than two-thirds of the Democrats opposing and more than two-thirds of the Republicans supporting Nixon's handling of the war.

Taking three major roll calls (the Cooper-Church amendment to curb future United States action in Cambodia, the Hatfield-Mc-Govern amendment to set a deadline for withdrawal of American forces from Vietnam, and an earlier procedural amendment by Democratic floor leader Mansfield, designed to head off opposition to the Hatfield-McGovern amendment), the proportion of antiwar votes out of total votes was as follows:

| Democrats | 78.3% antiwar votes |
| Republicans | 31.4% antiwar votes |

Some defection from party lines occurred, noticeably among southern Democrats and such Republicans as Brooke (Mass.), Case (N.J.), Cooper (Ky.), Hatfield (Ore.), and Javits (N.Y.). Yet a large majority in each party was clearly on opposite sides.

As the hostility or violence of the situation decreases, Presidential dominance in decision-making also decreases, with a corresponding increase in the congressional role. From an analysis of 22 cases, James Robinson concludes that Congress is more likely to be "highly involved" in nonviolent, as opposed to potentially or actually violent, cases and more likely to be "influential" in nonviolent cases.[6] That relationship will become clearer in the discussion of defense and foreign aid policies. But it can be seen also in the contrast between the declaring of war and the declaring of peace. In the Japanese Peace Treaty of 1952, the Senate "advised" as well as consented. During the preparation for the treaty, Ambassador Dulles met frequently with the Subcommittee on Far Eastern Affairs of the Senate Foreign Relations Committee. According to Bernard Cohen, the subcommittee participated in writing the provisions of the treaty to the extent of discussing and selecting from alternative proposals which Dulles presented.[7] The executive controlled the definition of alternatives, but the subcommittee influenced the choice of alternatives from those the executive selected. When the treaty was about to be submitted to the Senate, concern developed on the Senate floor that

---

[6] Robinson, op. cit., pp. 67, 68.

[7] Bernard Cohen, The Political Process and Foreign Policy: The Making of the Japanese Peace Settlement (Princeton: Princeton University Press, 1957).

Japan might negotiate a separate treaty with the Peiping government of China. Fifty-six senators, led by Senator William Knowland,
signed a letter to the President stating that unless assurance was
given on the point, they would oppose the treaty. Further discussions with the Japanese government, in which Senators Sparkman and
Smith of the subcommittee participated, brought written assurance
to the President from the Japanese prime minister that no such
treaty would be negotiated with Peiping. The Senate, after "advising" through its subcommittee system and through more widely
expressed senatorial concern, consented to the treaty.

Congressional concern with the status of American troops in the
NATO forces, lingering worries over United States participation in
the United Nations, and the growing use of Presidential "international agreements" in place of treaties lent support to a proposed
constitutional amendment initiated by Republican Senator Bricker
of Ohio in 1953. In its most controversial provisions, the amendment
sought to subject international agreements as well as treaties to
senatorial approval and to ensure that no treaty or other international agreement abrogated existing internal law: "A treaty or other
international agreement shall become effective as internal law in the
United States only through legislation by the Congress unless in
advising and consenting to a treaty the Senate, by a vote of two-
thirds of the Senate present and voting, shall provide that such
treaty may become effective as internal law without legislation by
the Congress."[8] The proposal was strongly opposed by Republican
President Eisenhower, who claimed it would "tie the President's
hands" in foreign policy-making. The closeness of the vote underlines the seriousness of the issue. When the Bricker amendment,
which was opposed by the Republican congressional leadership,
was defeated in the Senate 42 to 50 (R: 29–17; D: 13–32; I: 0–1),
an only slightly modified amendment was proposed by Senator
George of Georgia. Senator Knowland left his desk as majority
leader to announce support for the substitute amendment in opposi-

[8] *Congress and the Nation,* (Washington, D.C.: Congressional Quarterly,
Inc., 1965), p. 112.

tion to the Republican Presidential administration. Other congressional Republicans joined him. After intensive administration persuasion and last minute vote switching, the proposal fell one vote short of the two-thirds Senate majority it required, 60 to 31 (R: 32–14, D: 28–16; I: 0–1). One of the strongest assertions in recent years of congressional control over Presidential foreign policy-making had lost by one vote.

For a final illustration, during Kennedy's efforts to negotiate for a nuclear test ban treaty, the United States Senate posed at least as large a Presidential worry as the Russians. Congressional Republicans had long opposed Kennedy's "fuzzy-thinking disarmament advisers" and Republican Senate Leader Dirksen forecast that "a good many reservations would be presented."[9] The President's first fear was that enough southern Democrats, angered by his civil rights bill, would combine with Republicans to deny him the necessary two-thirds vote. Richard Russell, Chairman of the Senate Armed Services Committee, was opposed to the treaty and Washington's Senator Henry Jackson of the Armed Services Committee and the Joint Atomic Energy Committee reported that he and other members of the Armed Services Committee were "cautiously skeptical." Fortunately for the President's cause, the test ban, cast as a treaty, would be reported from the favorable Foreign Relations Committee. But even if the two-thirds vote could be managed, the second Presidential concern was for as wide a margin as possible. As Kennedy told a press conference, he did not want "only grudging support." In effect, he wanted the nation and the Senate in particular to support the President in peace with the unanimity it provides in war. To that end, an extensive Presidential campaign was mounted to solidify Senate support. While the Moscow talks were in session, Secretary of State Rusk was sent to brief the key committees and every senator was contacted and talked to on the subject. A bipartisan group of senators were invited on the delegation traveling to Moscow with Rusk for the official treaty-signing. (Republicans Dirksen and Hickenlooper declined.) The President took his

[9] Sorensen, op. cit., pp. 736–737.

case to the public. He encouraged organization of a "Citizens Committee for a Nuclear Test Ban" to mobilize public support, conduct extensive nationwide newspaper and television advertising, and see that specific senators heard from their constituents on the subject. By September 1963, when the Foreign Relations Committee favorably reported the treaty, Dirksen and other key senators had come out in support. But to illustrate the effect of a hostile committee, even one not charged with reporting the legislation, on the day the treaty went to the Senate floor Russell's Armed Services committee issued a report. The Preparedness Investigating Subcommittee of the Armed Services Committee had conducted secret hearings with Dr. Edward Teller and General Power, chief of the Strategic Air Command, both of whom opposed the test ban. The committee report concluded that the treaty involved "serious—perhaps formidable—military and technical disadvantages to the United States."[10]

In the resulting roll call, Kennedy got his extraordinary majority, with 55 Democrats and 25 Republicans voting yes, 11 Democrats (9 from the South, including Russell) and 8 Republicans, no. With impressive bipartisanship, the Senate finally rallied behind the President in a step toward peace. But its support was won at a high price of executive effort.

DEFENSE POLICY AND "REAL ESTATE"

Compared to decisions of war or other military commitment, the policy of defense and military "preparedness" involves increased congressional participation. However, it is participation of a specific kind and to a limited extent. It is still limited by executive dominance in expertise, control of information, and defining of alternatives and major goals. And it is shaped by what could be called a congressional consensus to approach defense policy from the viewpoint of domestic politics. That viewpoint itself has profound effects on the kind of policy that is made.

[10] *Congress and the Nation,* p. 135; Sorensen, *op. cit.,* pp. 734–740.

THE COMMITTEES

Congressional consideration of defense can be understood only within the committee structure and congressional norms of specialization, reciprocity, and seniority. The major defense committees are the House and Senate Armed Services committees, which handle the bulk of the substantive legislation on the subject, and the Defense Subcommittee of the House Appropriations Committee, which plays a decisive role in settling the yearly allocations for the defense budget. Both Armed Services committees, as an earlier chapter made clear, are senior, highly prestigious committees with low turnover of members. Chairmen in recent years have included Senator Richard Russell of Georgia and Representative Carl Vinson of Georgia, two of the most powerful men in the Congress. With such a membership, committee decisions will likely be accepted by the full Senate and House chambers, and therefore it is important to understand the committee's perception of its job, the factors that weigh heavily in *its* decisions, and the kind of policy that can be expected to result.

House Armed Services Committee members have expressed a limited view of their "policy-making" role. Members interviewed agreed first that their own expertise and information were limited and that they relied for advice and definition of alternatives on the Department of Defense and military expertise. As one influential member of the committee admitted: "How do we know what should be considered? We mostly reflect what the military people recommend; military policy is made by the Department of Defense. . . . So 95 percent of the legislation is what DOD recommends. . . ." Another said the same thing in almost the same words: "How the hell do we know what should be considered anyway? We mostly reflect what the military men tell us."[11] Members agreed, second, that what the committee did decide on was "real estate": questions of what

[11] Lewis Dexter, "Congressmen and the Making of Military Policy," in Robert Peabody and Nelson Polsby (eds), *New Perspectives on the House of Representatives* (2nd ed.; Skokie, Ill.: Rand McNally, 1969), pp. 181, 182, 185.

installations, where and how distributed; questions of the transfer and sale of properties; questions, it should be noted, most closely tied with congressional competence in representing their constituencies' interests and least involved with the major policy concerns. The norm of specialization buttresses constituency interest in defense and works against broader-ranging forays into areas of military expertise:

> Take bases. DOD says we need such-and-such bases. Well, we want to know why such-and-such a size. But we don't mostly know how to evaluate the answers; we aren't equipped to do so. . . . It's only when you come to personnel problems, size of army, that sort of thing, that you find us doing more—and that's naturally because that affects the lives of every voter.[12]

A staff member agreed: "Our committee is a real estate committee. Don't forget that. If you study our committee, you are studying real estate transactions."[13] A more independent stance appears to be taken by the Defense Subcommittee of the House Appropriations Committee, but the spectre of military expertise remains. Even in that committee, trained to guard the Treasury against executive "waste and error," is heard the plaguing question of congressional role: "Who are we to say 'no' to the military people?"[14] (Similar points are not raised of other experts. One does not hear "Who are we to say 'no' to the State Department? Or to IDA? Or to the economists?") The question was phrased rhetorically, but some may believe it deserves a thoughtful answer.

Whether the perceived incompetence is the guiding motive or whether it helps justify a supportive posture to defense decisions, one effect is the same. By and large, the key committees act not as a check but as a conduit for executive decisions, with the committee's decisions in turn accepted by the Senate and House. A decision *not* to make policy is itself a kind of policy. By restricting their role to allocating and distributing the costs and benefits of defense, the

12 *Ibid.,* p. 182.
13 *Ibid.,* p. 184.
14 *Ibid.*

committees place a stamp of approval on military policy made elsewhere.

Both Senate and House Armed Services committees are regionally representative, although they are well on the conservative side of congressional voting. (See Chapter 5.) Yet the committees are by no means "packed" in favor of a strong defense view. This point deserves careful attention. Committee members may have constituency defense installations to protect or aggrandize, but so do most non-committee members. The ABM controversy in the Ninety-first Congress, which split the Senate into liberal and conservative lines, with a majority of northern Democrats opposing a majority of southern Democrats and a majority of Republicans, also split the Senate committee in almost identical ratios—ND: 1–5, SD: 4–0, R: 5–3, in the committee's 10 to 8 vote for Nixon's ABM program. Congressional hawks may have been more attracted to the committees than congressional doves, but granting this one qualification the committees seem essentially representative of the Senate and House as a whole.

CONGRESSIONAL MEMBERSHIP

To the extent that there is a "pro-defense" outlook on the key committees, it is buttressed by wider congressional support. If Congress restricts its decisions to real estate transactions, defense issues can be translated into the more familiar questions of domestic politics concerning who gets what. While congressmen disclaim knowledge of esoteric military policy and weaponry, what they do claim is expert knowledge of their constituencies' interests. Many states and districts rely heavily on defense installations both for jobs and the overall well-being of the home economy. Many congressmen are "rated"—or at least perceive themselves as rated—by the share of the defense loaf they can bring home. In both his 1962 and 1968 bids for reelection, Wayne Morse was attacked by opponents on the ground that he did less for Oregon in the way of defense than other senators did for neighboring states: "Washington State's *working* senators won a billion dollars in military spending in one year for their people. . . . Oregon's *talking* senator has won only 6½ percent of what Washington received."[15] Other senators and representatives have compaigned explicitly on the defense spending they have "won . . . for their people." Note West Virginia Representative Ken Hechler's complaint in the House:

> I am firmly against the kind of logrolling which would subject our defense program to narrowly sectional or selfish pulling and hauling. But I am getting pretty hot under the collar about the way my state of West Virginia is shortchanged in Army, Navy, and Air Force installations. . . . I am going to stand up on my hind legs and roar until West Virginia gets the fair treatment she deserves.[16]

If defense is thus viewed as one of the largest loaves of domestic politics, the rules of distributive domestic politics apply. Constituency claims are represented. The norm of reciprocity is applied. It is true that some constituencies get more than others. When Georgia was represented by Armed Services Chairman Vinson in the House and Armed Services Chairman Russell in the Senate, the joke was made that one more base would sink the state. (Russell was also a member of the Joint Atomic Energy Committee and the Space Committee. He was subcommittee chairman of the Appropriations Subcommittee on Defense and member of the Appropriations Subcommittee on Military Construction.) But the loaf is distributed widely. Most districts have at least one military base or some defense-related industry. Thus the claim of "fairness" can be levied as in the Hechler complaint above: One man, one vote. One representative, one fair share of the United States defense establishment. Moreover and perhaps most importantly, it becomes virtually impossible to abolish old, obsolete commitments. One senior member of the Defense Subcommittee of the House Appropriations Committee summarized the problem:

> I am convinced defense is only one of the factors that enter into our determinations for defense spending. The others are pump priming, spreading the immediate benefits of defense spending, taking care of all services, giving all defense contractors a fair share, spreading the military

15 Editorial, *The Oregonian* (April 28, 1962), quoted by Douglas Cater, *Power in Washington* (New York: Random House, 1964), p. 39. Italics in original.
16 *Ibid.*, p. 38.

bases to include all sections, etc. . . . There is no state in the union and hardly a district in a state which doesn't have defense spending contracting, or a defense establishment. We see the effect in public and Congressional insistence on continuing contracts, or operating military bases though the need is expired.[17]

A cutback in a specific defense program means jobs, money—and quite possibly the congressman's job as well. Viewed in this light, congressional reciprocity working in the short run and incrementally has the profound long run aggregative effect of increasing the defense outlay and creating a certain programmatic inflexibility derived from the inability to rechannel once-committed resources.

The congressional deference to expertise should not be overstated. On occasion, Congress has opposed the executive, especially the Presidential, point of view. Congress has pressured the White House and the Department of Defense for continued production of manned bombers and for expanded development of missile and countermissile programs. It tried to stop President Truman from decreasing the size of the Marine Corps. In the Kennedy Administration, when Defense Secretary McNamara and top aides awarded the TFX seven billion dollar contract to General Dynamics over Boeing, Senator Jackson (of Washington, the chief base of Boeing) and his Senate committee undertook an investigation of the decision. Here was a case when a congressional committee investigation was launched against an executive decision. Congress, it seems, can jealously guard its prerogatives when prodefense decisions or particular allocations are at stake.

The 1962 issue of increased funds for the B-70 aircraft is another case in point. The House Armed Services Committee, supporting the Air Force and the industry against Kennedy and Defense Secretary McNamara's skepticism of the project, sought to dictate spending for a new RS-70 version of the old B-70 project. Previously the President had deliberately not spent the funds authorized by Congress. The 1962 authorization bill that emerged from Carl Vinson's committee reflected considerable institutional anger over this Presidential neglect of the congressional will. The bill "directed" the

17 *Ibid.*, p. 40.

President to spend nearly half a billion dollars—almost three times as much as Kennedy had requested—on the RS-70. It "ordered, mandated and required" that the full amount be spent. The provision continued:

> If the language constitutes a test as to whether Congress has the power to so mandate, let the test be made . . . [for] *the role of the Congress in determining national policy, defense or otherwise, has deteriorated over the years.*[18]

In this case the committee sought to enlarge the congressional role in defense policy in contrast to its usual, more deferential stance. Notice, however, that both assertive and restricted roles have been used to justify the same policy goal of increased defense spending. The wording of the bill threatened a constitutional issue over the separation of powers and a more immediate political problem: the Kennedy administration relied on Georgia's Vinson to gain Southern support for New Frontier proposals. In any event, Vinson was invited to the White House the day before House debate was scheduled to begin, and to the wonder of many, Vinson was persuaded to withdraw the test language.[19] The money was authorized, but the President was not explicitly "directed" or "mandated" to spend it. (It was never spent.)

In sum, Congress's normally restricted view of its role in defense has considerably wider policy ramifications. Restricting the congressional concern to real estate and employment for the constituency produces a policy resistant to change and committed to growth of the defense establishment. The committee system reinforces this effect and adds an independent effect of its own. When the Congress yields to its prestigious "expert" committees and these committees in turn yield to outside expertise (in this case military expertise), a supportive promilitary congressional policy is the result. And when Congress does undertake to assert its constitutional authority in opposition to the President, that more assertive stance is adopted with the same prodefense goal.

[18] Sorensen, *op. cit.,* pp. 347, 348. Italics added.
[19] *Ibid.,* p. 348.

Viewed in this light, the ABM debate in the Senate through both sessions of the Ninety-first Congress assumes greater importance. Nixon had to fight hard for his ABM program through a series of the narrowest victories: a 50 to 50 tie on a 1969 vote (the Vice-President cast the tie-breaking vote for the administration), and the slender margins of 52 to 47 and 53 to 45 in 1970 votes. Certainly in these roll calls and in the two-year debate that preceded them, the Senate did not exhibit a passive, prodefense role. The debate on ABM as on the war produced clear party lines, with 62.3 percent of the Democrats and 30.8 percent of the Republicans voting in four roll calls against the expanded ABM program. With such alignment, one can appreciate the difference that would have been made by some two to five more Democrats in the Senate.

Senate activity in the Ninety-first Congress may herald an increasingly active congressional role in war and defense, but the critical impact of public opinion cannot be ignored. Senate passivity or activity on questions of war and defense appears closely linked to a dormant or aroused public opinion. The normal pattern in the past was for the public and the Congress to "let the President do his job." If the Senate also has a "job" to do, public opinion must actively support it.

FOREIGN AID

Defense and foreign aid constitute two major sectors of American foreign policy that are subject to annual congressional legislation. Both are complex. Both involve division of powers between President and Congress. Both help shape "the American image" abroad. Against these similarities, the contrasts in congressional reaction are the more striking. Foreign aid cannot be translated into constituency jobs or real estate. Indeed, in constituency terms it tends to be seen as the reverse—as taxes. American citizens well-educated in the virtue of military preparedness have not been equally persuaded about the virtue of aid as preparedness for peace. Consequently, there is little constituency support for aid programs and no sizable vested congressional support. Indeed, there has been noticeable congressional opposition to Presidential aid programs. One does not hear the question of congressional role applied to aid—"Who are we to say no. . . ." Congress here appears to know what it is—an independent branch of government sharing responsibility for aid policy and representing different interests than the President. And it says no quite frequently. Since the Lend-Lease programs of the 1940s, Congress has lagged behind the executive on aid, as Presidents from Truman to Johnson have complained. Its general policy has been less aid, for less time, tied to more restraints, and more loans and fewer grants, with loans repayable in American dollars. Congress has expected appreciation from Western European recipients—concretely translated into support for United States foreign policy. It has been highly skeptical of aid to neutrals, and even more skeptical of aid to Communist states.

CONGRESSIONAL MEMBERSHIP: THE PARTIES

This is not to say there has been congressional unanimity on the subject. Support for aid programs from the 1940s through the 1960s varied considerably with party and region. Northern Democrats and a decreasing proportion of Republicans have represented the "internationalist" contingent of support for aid programs, while southern Democrats and the majority of Republicans have represented the more "isolationist" view of restricted aid, opposition to international "give away" programs, a harder line on aid to neutrals and nations in the Communist bloc. Southern Democratic opposition to aid was apparent by the mid-1950s, from which time to the present a majority of southerners opposed Presidential aid requests.[20] A majority of Republicans supported the Marshall Plan and its extension in the Truman years, but a majority opposed the mutual security program of 1951 and 1952. Republicans gave mixed support to Eisenhower's aid requests, but even these requests were considered inadequate by some pro-aid northern Democrats. By the 1960s as midwestern and western Republican opposition increased and the number of

[20] Holbert Carroll, *The House of Representatives and Foreign Affairs* (rev. ed.; Boston: Little, Brown, 1966), p. 356.

TABLE 7.1 Analysis of Key Congressional Roll Calls on Administration Foreign Aid Requests: Eighty-seventh and Eighty-eighth Congresses

ROLL CALL	PRESI-DENT'S STAND	VOTE (YEAS–NAYS)	VOTE BY PARTY[a]		VOTE BY REGION[a]	
Senate						
S 1983–Development Loan Fund: Ellender amendment to reduce authorization amount	No	51–43	D	21–39	ND	5–31
			R	30–4	SD	16–8
S 1983–Byrd amendment to require annual appropriations	No	39–56	D	16–46	ND	2–38
			R	23–10	SD	14–8
S 1983–Lausche amendment to reduce authorization amount	No	46–46[b]	D	20–40	ND	5–32
			R	26–6	SD	15–8
S 2000–Peace Corps Act: Hickenlooper amendment to reduce amount	No	32–59	D	8–51	ND	1–36
			R	24–8	SD	7–15
S 1215–Amend "Battle Act" of 1951 to increase President's discretion in aid recipients	Yes	43–36	D	36–18	ND	27–5
			R	7–18	SD	9–13
S 2214–International Development Association: Increase	Yes	38–31	D	28–16	ND	25–5
			R	10–15	SR	3–11
House						
HR 11921–Foreign Assistance Act: Increase	Yes	250–164	D	178–68	ND	135–9
			R	72–96	SD	43–59
HR 9022–International Development Association Increase: Recommit	No	208–189	D	71–161	ND	13–125
			R	137–28	SD	58–36
HR 9499–Jensen amendment to restrict loans to Communist countries	No	218–169	D	66–162	ND	16–117
			R	152–7	SD	50–45
HR 11812–Appropriations: Rhodes motion to recommit and reduce	No	198–208	D	55–185	ND	8–135
			R	143–23	SD	47–50

[a] Partisan and regional majorities are in italics.
[b] The amendment was rejected. Vice-President Johnson did not have to cast the deciding vote.

southern Republicans increased, Republican majorities were firmly on the opposition side.[21]

[21] *Ibid.*, p. 357.

Given these alignments by party and region, the composition of committees dealing with aid questions and the pattern of House and Senate voting on Presidential requests have helped shape American aid policy through the past three decades. Notice the congressional response to key aid legislation proposed by Kennedy, of all the recent Presidents probably the one most interested in an expanded aid program as an instrument of foreign policy. The roll calls in the House and Senate were *party votes,* defined as votes where a majority of one party opposed a majority of the other party. Moreover, most issues split the Democratic party into North and South, with a majority of southern Democrats voting with a majority of Republicans against Kennedy and the majority of northern Democrats. The stability of alignments on Kennedy's major aid proposals is vividly demonstrated in Table 7.1.

As the table makes clear, the President won on some requests and lost on others, depending on the number of southern Democratic and Republican defections from party. All of the votes listed, which are representative of major aid questions in the 1960s, are party votes. All but two show a regional split in northern and southern majorities within the Democratic party. The consistent pattern of opposing majorities for both party and region is striking. From the 1950s to the present, the Midwest and West were consistently pro-aid in Democratic congressional voting and consistently anti-aid in Republican voting. Since the congressmen from these regions comprised more than one-third of the House and approximately one-half of the Senate, it is clear that whether Republicans or Democrats were elected in these states and districts made a profound difference in outcomes in foreign aid legislation.

THE COMMITTEES

Floor voting, of course, is only one part of congressional policymaking, and many Presidential roll call "victories" may be weak compromises compared to original requests. A large part of congressional aid policy is shaped in committee.

The Senate Foreign Relations Committee is charged with initiating most substantive aid legislation and with authorizing appropriations bills. A highly prestigious committee, Foreign Relations has enjoyed a stable membership through recent years and a membership more liberal, more "international," and more favorable to foreign aid than the Senate average. A comparison of committee members to nonmembers for the Eightieth through the Eighty-fourth Congress (1947 through 1956) on an "internationalism"-"anti-internationalism" dimension found committee members voting more frequently for foreign aid and other expressions of "internationalism" than their noncommittee colleagues.[22] For a follow-up study, Table 7.2 reports the average number of *pro-aid* votes per congressman out of five key Senate roll calls in Kennedy's Eighty-seventh Congress for com-

CONGRESS	80TH	81ST	82ND	83RD	84TH	TOTAL
No. of roll calls	8.0	14.0	13.0	7.0	7.0	49.0
Average no. of anti-international votes per committee member	0	0.8	0.8	0.9	0.7	0.6
Average no. of anti-international votes per non-committee member	1.9	3.5	3.5	2.2	1.2	2.5

TABLE 7.2 Comparative Support for Aid Programs of Senate Foreign Relations Committee Members and Nonmembers: Eighty-seventh Congress[a]

	AVERAGE NO. OF PRO-AID VOTES PER SENATOR (OUT OF 5 VOTES)			
	COMMITTEE MEMBERS		NONMEMBERS	
	N	PRO-AID VOTES	N	PRO-AID VOTES
Democrats	(9)	3.8	(51)	3.2
Northern Democrats	(5)	4.0	(31)	4.2
Southern Democrats	(4)	3.5	(20)	1.8
Republicans	(5)	1.4	(25)	1.2
Total	(14)	2.9	(76)	2.5

[a] The five key votes selected from the Eighty-seventh Congress were scheduled in Table 7.1: the three roll calls on the Foreign Assistance Act of 1961 (S 1983), the Hickenlooper amendment to reduce the Peace Corps authorization (S 2000), and the amendment to the "Battle Act" of 1951 (S 1215).

22 David Farnsworth, "A Comparison of the Senate and its Foreign Relations Committee on Selected Roll-Call Votes," *Western Political Quarterly* (1961): 173.

mittee members and nonmembers. (Only senators voting on at least four of the five roll calls were included.) While committee members overall exhibit somewhat higher support for aid than nonmembers, it is the southern Democrats that make the difference. Northern Democrats and Republicans on the committee appear to be representative of their congressional parties on aid policy. But the southern Democratic noncommittee members, averaging a weak 1.8 pro-aid votes out of 5, are represented on the committee by southern colleagues averaging 3.5 pro-aid votes out of 5.

By the Ninety-first Congress, the three most recent Republican additions included Case, Javits, and Cooper—all liberals and supporters of foreign aid. With southern Democrats and a number of Republicans on the committee voting with the northern Democrats, the pro-aid view has carried in committee decisions.

The House Foreign Affairs Committee is less prestigious than its Senate counterpart and subject to more rapid turnover as members leave for more attractive assignments. According to one study, its chairmen—totalling six in the past twenty years—have not been particularly influential in the House and have not sought an active role for the committee.[23] But like the Senate committee, House Foreign Affairs members have been slightly more supportive of aid than noncommittee members. Table 7.3 compares the two House groups for key roll calls in the Eighty-eighth Congress. Note in particular the Republican overpresentation of aid supporters. The Eighty-eighth Congress produced a systematic attempt by the Republican leadership to appoint opponents of aid to the committee.[24] Five of the six new Republican appointees had consistently opposed aid programs in the past congresses and continued to do so as committee members. (Representatives Gross, Berry, Derwinski, Battin, and Thompson gave a total of 0 votes in support of the roll calls analyzed in Table 7.3. Morse of Massachusetts, a pro-aid Republican, was the sixth appointee.) So apparently the committee was

[23] Carroll, *op. cit.*, pp. 30, 90–109.
[24] *Ibid.*, p. 355.

TABLE 7.3 Comparative Support for Aid Programs of House Foreign Affairs Committee Members and Nonmembers: Eighty-eighth Congress[a]

| | AVERAGE NO. OF PRO-AID VOTES PER REPRESENTATIVE (OUT OF 3 VOTES) | | | |
| | COMMITTEE MEMBERS | | NONMEMBERS | |
	N	PRO-AID VOTES	N	PRO-AID VOTES
Democrats	(19)	2.5	(227)	2.1
Northern Democrats	(14)	2.9	(134)	2.5
Southern Democrats	(5)	1.2	(93)	1.3
Republicans	(13)	.9	(160)	.3
Total	(32)	1.8	(387)	1.3

[a] The three roll calls for the Eighty-eighth Congress used were reported in Table 7.1. They include a motion to recommit the authorization bill for the IDA (HR 9022), the Hensen amendment barring the Export-Import Bank from lending to Communist countries (HR 9499), and the Rhodes motion to the appropriations bill to recommit and reduce (HR 11812). Only Representatives voting on two of the three roll calls were included in the analysis.

even more supportive of aid programs in congresses before the Eighty-eighth.

While the two substantive committees have offered no obstacle to Presidential aid requests, there is another committee which must be dealt with: the House Appropriations Committee and in particular, its Subcommittee on Foreign Operations. Under the full committee chairmanship of Clarence Cannon, the subcommittee was headed by Otto Passman. Passman, a pronounced foe of foreign aid, packed the committee with likeminded members who together worked to cut Presidential aid requests to the barest minimum. Since a strong committee norm of specialization operates in Appropriations, subcommittee decisions tend to be accepted by the full committee, whose decisions are accepted by the House. The influence of the subcommittee chairman under such a scheme is obvious. Theodore Sorensen summarizes Passman's role in the Kennedy aid programs as follows:

Appropriations Subcommittee Chairman Otto Passman of Louisiana felt *his* annual responsibility was to cut back foreign aid as sharply as possible. Immune to the President's personal pleas, and aided by members of both parties . . . Passman had no difficulty in finding examples of waste and error. . . . Each year Kennedy lost more ground to Passman.[25]

On Cannon's death in 1964, George Mahon of Texas became chairman. Mahon, in the words of Holbert Carroll, "proved to be less tolerant of the subcommittee's foreign policy-making propensities" than his predecessor.[26] And he—not Passman—took charge of subcommittee assignments. He added two northern Democratic aid supporters and the moderate Clarence Long of Maryland and dropped two southern Democrats from the subcommittee. Note the results, as measured by votes on the three aid roll calls of the Eighty-eighth Congress. (See Table 7.4.) Passman no longer had "his" majority on the subcommittee. Opponents of aid dropped from 7 out of 11 to 4 out of 9 members. The Mahon subcommittee arrangement, still chaired by Passman, has remained in effect through the Ninety-first Congress.

TABLE 7.4 Aid Voting of Foreign Operations Subcommittee Members: Eighty-eighth and Eighty-ninth Congresses Compared

CANNON SUBCOMMITTEE (88th Congress)	VOTES (PRO-AID– ANTI-AID)	MAHON SUBCOMMITTEE (89th Congress)	VOTES (PRO-AID– ANTI-AID)
Democrats		*Democrats*	
Passman, La.	1–2	Passman, La.	1–2
Gary, Va.	1–2	Rooney, N.Y.	3–0
Rooney, N.Y.	3–0	Natcher, Ky.	2–1
Natcher, Ky.	2–1	Hansen, Wash.	2–0
Andrews, Ala.	0–3	Cohelan, Calif.	2–0
Montoya, N.M.	1–2	Long, Md.	1–2
Flynt, Ga.	3–0		
Republicans		*Republicans*	
Rhodes, Ariz.	0–2	Shriver, Kans.	0–3
Ford, Mich.	1–2	Conte, Mass.	3–0
Conte, Mass.	3–0	Andrews, N.D.	0–2
Minshall, Ohio	0–3		
47% pro-aid votes		58% pro-aid votes	

[25] Sorensen, *op. cit.*, p. 351.
[26] Carroll, *op. cit.*, p. 354.

CONGRESS AND FOREIGN AID

What has been the effect of all this—the role of parties, the changing composition of Senate and House membership, the membership and chairmen of the key committees—on United States foreign aid in recent decades? In what ways and to what critical extent has Congress shaped aid policy? Presidential initiative in the area is clear. The ideas have been executive in inspiration, Their support has been Presidential. Milestones in aid have been set by American Presidents and, with sufficiently large Presidential effort at persuasion, Congress has agreed: the 1947 Truman Doctrine, the Marshall Plan, Kennedy's Alliance for Progress.

Quite clearly also, by giving qualified (in some cases grudging) responses, Congress has set limits defining the range of Presidential initiative. Its limit-setting role is clearest for the levels of aid. Presidential aid requests may serve as the initial talking point, but levels are set through interbranch and interhouse monetary bargaining, with the Appropriations subcommittee setting the minimum level for debate. The effect of this limit-setting may be seen in President Johnson's "bare bones" request for foreign aid in fiscal 1965. After a 33.8 percent cut in the Kennedy program the preceding year, the largest reduction since the beginning of aid programs in 1948, Johnson asked Congress to appropriate some 3.4 billion for foreign economic and military aid—1.1 billion below Kennedy's 1964 request. Passman still sought to reduce the figure by $515 million, but the new Mahon subcommittee, for the first time in Passman's ten years as subcommittee chairman, did not support him and reduced the Johnson figure by only $200 million.[27] The final record low cut of 7.6 percent may be seen in part as a response to a President's more realistic view of aid support in Congress and in part as a result of the reshuffled subcommittee.

Congress has set qualitative as well as quantitative limits. It has denied aid to Communist nations, and to nations selling strategic goods to the Soviet Union or Cuba, with profound effects on United States foreign policy. And at times Congress has specifically selected

[27] *Congress and The Nation*, p. 185.

recipients and nonrecipients of aid. It has debated aid to Spain and aid to Poland. In 1950, against the known opposition of the Truman administration, it authorized aid for Spain. Given Truman's delicate relations with the Eighty-first Congress on other matters, the program was actually implemented by the reluctant administration. (Senator Pat McCarran who introduced the amendment was a personal friend of Franco. Also, Spanish anticommunism impressed the Congress.[28]) It has prohibited aid to nations (United Arab Republic) preparing for military action against a nation (Israel) receiving American aid. It has cut off assistance to Indonesia. Besides selecting aid recipients, it has set specific terms. By denying Presidential requests for long-term borrowing and insisting on annual appropriations, it has forced the executive to a year-by-year process of bargaining and review and forced foreign economies into short-run planning. It has at times required one-half of aid shipments to be transported by American-flag vessels. It has dictated the currency for repayment of loans, set Export-Import Bank lending policy, and frequently suggested to foreign nations the kinds of uses to which aid funds should be directed. Since Presidents have had to bargain for any viable aid program at all, Congress has enjoyed leverage on these specific points of policy.

SUMMARY

One chapter in a book of this size and scope cannot give full justice to congressional participation in foreign policy in the recent years. It cannot even cover the range of separate policy areas: for example, United States trade policy, atomic energy policy, or sharing of information with other nations. What the chapter has attempted is to trace the differing share of influence between legislative and executive in three policy areas and to demonstrate in those areas of relatively greater congressional involvement how the membership and organization affect the policy that is made. The discussion has

[28] Louis W. Koenig, "Foreign Aid to Spain and Yugoslavia," in Alan Westin (ed.), *The Uses of Power* (New York: Harcourt Brace Jovanovich, 1962), pp. 73–116.

traced successively increasing congressional involvement—from decisions of war or other military action to decisions about peace, to defense policy, to the politics of foreign aid. Defense and aid, it will be seen, have much in common with the domestic policies analyzed in the following chapter. As crisis subsides and information and participation become less restricted, as the patterns and predispositions of domestic policies increase, congressional influence grows stronger. And as it grows, party and constituency loyalties, congressional norms, and the members and chairmen of the key committees grow in importance. American foreign aid is shaped in part by the committee and subcommittee chairmen of the House Appropriations Committee. Defense programs are won or lost by the number of Democrats or Republicans voting on the floor. Norms of specialization and reciprocity make defense policy into real estate. And specialization, seniority, and the committee system have made Georgia what it is today. These influences have been documented only at a few isolated points of time. Much remains to be done, especially in exploring changes over time. But the documentation should be sufficient to stimulate further study.

It is an intriguing fact that in the foreign policy sphere Congress has been criticized both with doing too much and too little. Involvement has been "meddling," and lack of involvement "parochialism." It has been damned if it did and damned if it didn't. It has been criticized also for the kind of activity it has engaged in. Decision-making has been low-level and incremental. Congress has left to the President and his advisers on affairs of defense and state the making of major policy—the critical, the large, and the long-term decisions. It has occupied itself with the details and follow-up decisions on how much and where. The committee structure divides deliberation into a number of different committees and subcommittees. The norm of specialization further reinforces the specific, the limited, the low-level view. Appropriations decisions on aid and defense, which offer opportunity for broad evaluation of policy, have concentrated instead on incremental raises or cuts and the search for waste and error in specific programs. Perhaps most of all, it has concentrated on the domestic politics involved in aid and defense. Parties have provided some general frame for organizing congressional views and in so doing have facilitated a consistency in congressional policy over time. Beyond party, congressional interest has mirrored constituency interest—the lack of enthusiasm for or skepticism about foreign aid, the fear of Communism, the concern for an adequate defense, and the American competitive instinct to "beat the Russians" in missiles, space, or any other game. At times it has mirrored specific constituency interests—a dying naval base, an economy tied to manned bombers, a new aircraft development. At times it has mirrored the public's lack of interest. But in ideology or real estate and through all its action including the lack of action, it is difficult to avoid the conclusion that Congress has been representative of a wider American public view. It may be criticized, basically, because it represents so well.

CHAPTER 8

PARTIES, COMMITTEES, AND POLICY-MAKING

*I*n domestic policy Congress is quite literally on its home ground. But, as in foreign policy, its influence varies with Presidential interest and initiative and the extent of public concern. According to current expectations, Congress looks to the President for initiation of new programs. His State of the Union address, his messages to Congress, and his nationally televised speeches define the priorities and main agenda for the congressional session. Priorities are translated into more concrete terms by Presidential budget allocations as worked out by the Bureau of the Budget. An administration bill may be torn apart and put together again by a congressional committee; nevertheless, it is the administration bill that supplies the basic talking point. Presidential interest may "raise up" an issue to national—and congressional— consideration. Foreign aid and trade (Kennedy) or ABM and the politics of Supreme Court nominations (Nixon) may command conspicuous Presidential interest in one administration but in another be handled routinely and less visibly when other interests predominate. Initiative, prestige, and the publicity available to the office give the President considerable effectiveness as chief legislator.

The President's influence may be limited only by his interest and his political currency in the country, but it *is* limited by these. For every issue singled out for Presidential attention, scores of others are decided elsewhere. A single executive may watch only one or two issues at a time. The congressional committee structure is ideally suited for the watching of many. Specific publics, represented by specific congressmen on key committees, can translate their own interest into influence. And a widely aroused public opinion, transmitted into congressional opinion, can counter even Presidential indifference.

On the congressional side, the specialized interests of committee members can profoundly affect policy. The most frequently cited case is the negative interest of the chairman or committee majority in blocking legislation. But even in legislation recommended by the committee, committee alignments may set the terms for subsequent floor debate. Committee interest shapes the extent and kind of congressional oversight given to programs. And in some cases, committee specialists may innovate and initiate new national policy.

Party membership in Congress is also critical to the success of specific policies, including Presidential programs. Congressional Republicans and Democrats took consistent and opposing stands on a number of major domestic issues during the 1947–1968 period. Social welfare issues, such as education, housing, medical care, and poverty, found Democrats consistently favoring the program and Republicans opposing. Fiscal policy, labor, farm supports, conservation issues involving the extent of the federal government's role, similarly found the parties sharply and consistently opposed. Of course, some large portion of southern Democrats have regularly voted with the Republicans and a small number of Republicans have voted with the northern Democrats on many of these issues. The continuing existence of the conservative coalition from the late 1930s to the present has blurred party lines. And further, as noted in Chapter 3, most congressmen are obliged to defect from party on some issues of specific constituency concern. Nevertheless, given the overall importance of party in organizing congressional opinion on policy plus the possibility of defection, it is clear that the underlying partisan strength in Congress—that is the gross number of partisans representing potential support for policies—can, in large part, shape patterns of compromise and ultimate passage or defeat.

It should be clear that no single chapter can pretend to cope with all this variety and complexity. The subject is huge, and existing policy studies are scant. All that can be done is to select some cases from the limited studies available to illustrate the variation and extent of congressional influence and the impact of party and committee membership in the process. This attempt, at least, can demonstrate the impact on policy of the membership and organization as analyzed in earlier chapters.

FEDERAL AID TO EDUCATION

Federal aid-to-education bills have been sponsored and supported at the Presidential level, yet few policies demonstrate as clearly as this the limits of Presidential leverage vis-à-vis the Congress. A "new" program in the 1950s, when education was considered a state and local concern, aid to education had relatively small support in Congress compared to more established programs. Political parties helped to organize opinion on the issue, but the parties' organizing effect was limited by constituency interest. Republicans consistently opposed federal aid, with the exception of a few northeastern urban mavericks, but the Democratic party split on the issues. Southern opposition increased with the emergence, after 1954, of the issue of aid to segregated schools. The religious issue raised by the question of aid to nonpublic schools split off key Democrats from the urban Northeast. Year after year Presidents sent education bills to the Congress and year after year the conservative coalition managed to stop them there.

Aid to education, like civil rights and poverty bills in the two post-World War II decades, called for innovative legislation. As such, these proposals found first access in the Presidency, evoking only minority support in Congress along with strong minority opposition. With the legislative process organized as a series of stages, each requiring majority support for passage, it can be contended that by its very nature any innovative legislation of whatever ideological stamp faces built-in difficulty in the Congress. Committees work partially in cooperation with party leaders to screen proposals for floor consideration. Thus the major site for negative congressional decisions on innovative legislation is the committee stage.

THE COMMITTEES

Through the 1950s the negative decision on aid to education was made by the House Education and Labor Committee, whose composition and leadership were described in Chapter 5. The conflict on the committee has worked against the reporting of new and controversial legislation. With membership systematically selected and self-selected on issue lines, the committee has concentrated in its membership the domestic political conflict in the House. Partisan lines divide the committee, more sharply on the issue of federal role than they divide the House. Compared to 1961 average percentages among House Democrats of 78 percent in favor of a larger federal role and 21 percent against, committee Democrats averaged 91 percent in favor and 8 percent against. House Republicans averaged 12 percent in favor and 87 percent against, compared to committee Republicans who averaged 7 percent for, 93 percent against.[1] Added to the polarization by party, conflict on education issues has split the Democrats on the committee. As one Republican member described it, "They'll shout at each other, stand up and bang their fists on the table and stomp out." And a Democratic member agreed: "Our executive sessions are the most exciting things you ever saw."[2]

Until the Eighty-sixth Congress a thin conservative majority plus the active assistance of Chairman Barden worked against the reporting of education bills. In 1947 and 1948, the Senate twice passed school aid bills only to have legislation stopped in the House committee. Through the 1950s, legislation similarly was stopped in the House committee, in part through the obstructionist tactics of the chairman. Following the Democratic House victory of 1958, the strengthened liberal Democrats pressured Speaker Rayburn for a new party ratio on the committee in the Eighty-sixth congress of 20 Democrats to 10 Republicans (the ratio had been 17 to 13). Six new Democrats were added. None were from the South. All were

[1] Richard F. Fenno, Jr., "The House of Representatives and Federal Aid to Education," in Robert L. Peabody and Nelson W. Polsby (eds.), New Perspectives on the House of Representatives (2nd ed.; Skokie, Ill.: Rand McNally, 1969), p. 292.
[2] Ibid., p. 286.

staunch liberals and firm supporters of aid to education. With the change in committee membership, the conservative majority was eliminated, the revolt against Chairman Barden occurred, and education bills began to pass through the substantive committee stage. But the Rules Committee remained to be reckoned with. Rules had lost two moderate Republicans whom party leader Halleck replaced by firm conservatives. The result was that Rules, widely reputed to be more conservative in its Democratic membership than the House Democrats as a whole, was even more strongly conservative in its Republican membership than the House Republicans as a whole. Whereas House Republicans and Education and Labor Republicans both averaged 74 percent in support of the conservative coalition in the Eighty-sixth Congress, Rules Committee Republicans averaged 93 percent. House Democrats averaged 32 percent; Education and Labor Democrats averaged a liberal low of 12 percent; and Rules Committee Democrats were slightly more conservative than the House Democrats with 39 percent in support. When the Senate passed a school aid bill, the companion House version was reported out by the House Education and Labor Committee overriding Barden. It was left to die in Rules. A school construction bill was finally extricated from Rules after the discharge procedure was launched. That bill passed the House but never reached the conference stage, again because of the Rules Committee's obstructive action. In sum, education bills had been submitted in the House in every Congress from the Seventy-ninth through the Eighty-sixth. None were passed. For most of the period, the House committees of Education and Rules were the decisive site for the negative decision on education.[3]

COMMITTEE AND FLOOR: 1961

The Eighty-seventh Congress brought the advent of a new Democratic administration in the White House and a "liberalized" Rules Committee. Liberal Democrats finally pressured Speaker Rayburn

[3] For a summary chart of House action on aid to education bills, see Frank Munger and Richard Fenno, *National Politics and Federal Aid to Education* (Syracuse: Syracuse University Press, 1962), p. 9.

into moving for an increase in the committee's size from 12 to 15 members. After a House fight the increase was voted, 217 to 212. The three additional members included two Democrats—Carl Elliot, an Alabama liberal on domestic policy (exclusive of civil rights), and B. F. Sisk, a California liberal—and one Republican conservative. The change gave the nonconservatives on the committee a paper thin 8 to 7 majority and brought the Democratic ideological composition of the committee into line with that of the Democratic House. (Whereas Rules Democrats voted on the average 31 percent in support of the conservative coalition in the Eighty-seventh Congress, House Democrats voted 30 percent in support.)[4]

With a Democratic President, a slightly liberalized Rules Committee, and the replacement of Barden by Adam Clayton Powell as chairman of the Education and Labor Committee, the situation looked more favorable for an education bill. The administration bill passed the favorable Senate committee and was approved by the Senate, 49 to 34, with southern Democrats splitting for and against the bill. It was reported from the House substantive committee only to be enmired in the Rules Committee on the issue of aid to parochial schools. Two Catholic Democrats on Rules joined the Republicans and conservative Democrats to transform the thin proeducation majority back into a minority. Rules delayed hearings on the bill. When the proeducation forces tried to extract the bill from Rules under Calendar Wednesday proceedings, the motion to consider was defeated by the House, 242 to 170.[5] Once again, a school aid bill passed by the Senate did not survive the House.

Explanations for the defeat must include the inability to resolve the parochial school issue, the impact of the Rules Committee, and

[4] That newly won similarity between House and Rules Committee Democrats persisted through the Eighty-ninth Congress. By the Ninetieth Congress, the Rules Democrats were *more* liberal than the House Democrats (22 percent compared to 32 percent in support of the conservative coalition). The Rules Republicans in the Ninetieth Congress remained more conservative than House Republicans (79 percent compared to 70 percent in support).

[5] See Hugh Douglas Price, "Race, Religion, and the Rules Committee: The Kennedy Aid-to-Education Bills," in Alan F. Westin (ed.), *The Uses of Power* (New York: Harcourt Brace Jovanovich, 1962), pp. 1–72.

the expected strength of House southern Democrats and Republicans voting in opposition. Douglas Price's analysis of the outcome includes one additional factor—the lack of Presidential leadership. Price argues that Kennedy never really fought for the education bill. Other programs had his attention. Thus foreign aid was also under consideration during the education fight, and members of the two foreign affairs committees, rather than those involved in the education bill, received the invitations to the White House. According to Price:

> The President was simply not prepared to jeopardize his whole legislative program . . . by a bitter fight to the death for aid to education. . . . The Administration had deliberately refrained from endorsing civil rights legislation in order to facilitate passage of other parts of his program. Similarly, the President apparently decided to knuckle under on aid to education. He could not win every round against the conservative coalition in the House.[6]

Compare this account with the description in Chapter 7 of Kennedy's efforts on the foreign aid bill, which he won in part, though he won less than he had hoped for. Given limited Presidential priorities, the composition of the House membership not only can vote specific Presidential proposals up or down; it also sets parameters for what will be proposed and for how much will be attempted.

COMMITTEE AND FLOOR: 1965

With the 1964 Johnson landslide, the House gained 38 new Democratic members, predominantly from the North, for a strong 295 to 140 margin over the Republicans in the Eighty-ninth Congress. With the change in membership, party ratios changed on the committees. House Education and Labor, presumably with the help of the Democratic party leadership, added five new Democrats, all of whom had campaigned on the school aid issue.[7] Of two new Republicans, one was proeducation, producing a stronger margin of sup-

---

[6] *Ibid.*, pp. 65–68.

[7] Eugene Eidenberg and Ray Morey, *An Act of Congress* (New York: Norton, 1969), p. 49. For importance of the committee membership to passage, see p. 51.

port for education forces on the committee. The new liberal House majority reinstated the 21-day Rule to limit the obstructive impact of Rules. As passed at the beginning of the Eighty-ninth Congress, the 21-day Rule allowed the Speaker to recognize committee members to call for House consideration of legislation kept in the Rules Committee for 21 days. As Chairman Howard Smith of Rules predicted gloomily, "the skids were being greased." Rules could not be used in the Eighty-ninth as it had on other occasions to block legislation that the party leadership desired. With a proeducation committee, a restrained Rules Committee, and a liberal House majority, all earlier congressional obstructions to an education bill were removed. Johnson's bill passed the House committee and was reported, 8 to 7, by the Rules Committee. (The 21-day threat remained in the background in case of an unfavorable vote.) Johnson's bill received the full efforts of the Democratic party leadership in mobilizing floor support and passed the House, 263 to 153.[8] After Senate passage it was signed into law.

The importance of the party membership change in the Eighty-ninth Congress cannot be overstated. It brought a comfortable margin of support for education on the key committees and on the floor as new liberal Democrats took their places as voting members —even if they were not expected to stay. It brought a 21-day Rule, which further facilitated action by the new majority—even if it also was not expected to stay. (When those new liberal Democrats *left* Congress after the 1966 election, the 21-day Rule was swiftly repealed.) Add to the effect of membership the Presidential skill and effort which kept party defections to a minimum, education policy was not uniquely affected. Democratic party proposals, pushed since the Truman administration with limited to zero degrees of success, were enacted into law by the Eighty-ninth Congress.

What happened after the 1966 elections provides the best comment on the long-run impact of such initial victories. The Johnson Administration sent another school aid bill to the Ninetieth Congress, which had lost its luxurious margin of Democrats and had

[8] *Ibid.*, pp. 119–126.

repealed the 21-day Rule. Aid to education was passed in 1967 by compromising extensively with the Republicans on the form such aid should take. But a bill was passed, and the administration scored at least a partial victory. Aid programs continued. Eidenberg and Morey comment on the "new level" of education debate after the first education bill in the Eighty-ninth Congress had been fought and won. While some firm old-line opposition to any school aid persisted, "in recent years . . . leaders on both sides no longer quibble about the basic concept. Controversy now centers on the amount and means of distribution."[9] Maintaining support in Congress, it would seem, is easier than winning it in the first place. And as a program continues and stabilizes relationships among congressmen, executive participants, and clientele, such support grows stronger.

With new programs, attention turns to the Presidency. It is the President's choice, in part depending on his reading of priorities and the events of the time, that determines which new programs will be pushed hardest and which can be sacrificed for others. It is the President's skill as party leader working in conjunction with congressional leaders that may hold the line against defections. Past Presidential election results as they affect congressional elections help shape the critical margin of partisan support. Congressional membership shapes the party and committee structures, which will help determine outcomes and sets parameters for Presidential expectations. An innovative President may need to push and push a skeptical or uninterested Congress for a new program, which by its being new does not have well-established congressional support. But once won, the same battle usually need not be fought again.[10]

PARTIES, INTERESTS, AND AGRICULTURE

In contrast to the education controversy, the politics of agriculture has been comparatively stable and well defined. It has divided

[9] *Ibid.*, p. 213.
[10] Exceptions can be found, such as Johnson's Highway Beautification bill passed in the Eighty-ninth Congress. The program was voted no funds in the first session of the Ninetieth Congress and only minimal funds in the second session.

Congress into two blocs: one favoring high price supports, general assistance to farmers, and strict production controls; the other favoring lower supports calculated by different means and few production limitations. Even more clearly than the 1967 education bill, the conflict has centered on the amount and means of distribution. The issue of price supports, battled in Congress after Congress from the 1940s well into the 1960s, shows more clearly than most issues the influence of constituency interest, the attention of attentive publics, and the organizing, mobilizing force of the political parties.

MEMBERSHIP

The core of the high-support bloc was composed of southern and western Democrats representing areas of heavy farm population and relatively poor small farmers who, faced with high production costs, needed guaranteed high price levels. In the South especially, the concentration on specific commodities such as cotton, tobacco, and peanuts meant that sharp price drops for these three crops would bring severe economic loss throughout the region. Plains Republicans from wheat-growing states also favored high supports. They argued that the inelastic demand for wheat meant that lower prices would not increase sales. The low-support bloc included congressmen from the rural North Central, and northeastern Republicans from dairying and poultry areas, who needed to buy feed grains at low prices, some western congressmen from cattle areas, and Republican congressmen from the corn belt. Thus congressmen on both the high and low support sides could perceive a "policy constituency" actively and homogeneously concerned with the policy under consideration.[11] These comprised the "interested" congressmen from interested constituencies.

Attentive publics included the heavy proportion of farmers in the voting population and representatives of organized farm groups. The National Farmers Union (NFU) favored high government supports for farmers, strict production controls, and price supports.

[11] Charles O. Jones, "Representation in Congress; The Case of the House Agriculture Committee," *American Political Science Review* (June 1961): 358–367.

Its opposite number, the American Farm Bureau Federation by the late 1940s began advocating removal of production controls and reduced price support levels. Both groups were supported by a large farm membership and worked closely with the farmers. They constituted a major political influence on congressmen from constituencies where Bureau or NFU membership was strong.[12]

THE COMMITTEES

Agriculture policy illustrates in sharpest relief the use of the committee system for constituency representation. Congressmen from interested farm constituencies almost without exception have comprised the membership of House and Senate agriculture committees. (The Democrats traditionally drafted one loyal New York City member to represent "consumer interests" on the House committee.) Charles Jones' study of the 1958 House committee found the following membership as defined by their constituencies' chief commodities:[13]

House Agriculture Committee

Democrats		Republicans	
Tobacco	7	Wheat	3
Cotton and Rice	6	Corn	5
Dairy	2	Dairy	3
Corn	1	Diversified	4
Diversified	2		

The Democrats' "diversified" members included Victor Anfuso, of Brooklyn.

Constituency representation in the committee is reinforced by heavy reliance on subcommittees. Subcommittees are organized by commodity, with the membership distributed into subcommittees

---

[12] See Theodore Lowi, "How the Farmers Get What They Want," *The Reporter* (May 21, 1964): 34–37. See also the Editors of the *Yale Law Journal*, "The Political Impasse in Farm Support Legislation," in Randall B. Ripley (ed.), *Public Policies and Their Politics* (New York: Norton, 1966), pp. 69–78.

[13] Jones, *op. cit.*

according to the constituency's chief commodity interest. It is true that both parties need to appoint some uninterested members to subcommittees (Republicans, on the cotton subcommittee, Democrats, on wheat). But a norm of constituency interest pervades subcommittee deliberation. As Jones reports from interviews: "members who have little interest in the proceedings are expected either to remain silent during hearings or not to attend."[14]

With this "interested" committee membership, much of the politics of agriculture can be decided by interaction between representatives of commodity interests, the committee members, and executive agency personnel. Cater calls the arrangement a "subgovernment." Theodore Lowi calls it a "triangular trading pattern" in which "each side of the triangle complements and supports the other two." According to Lowi's account of specific triangular systems, one includes the Extension Service, the "farm-bureau" members of the agriculture committees, and the American Farm Bureau Federation with its local committees. Another involves the Soil Conservation Service, the Agriculture Subcommittee of the House Appropriations Committee, and the local districts organized into the National Association of Soil Conservation Districts. Another, concerned with price supports, involves the Agricultural Stabilization and Conservation Service with the eight commodity subcommittees of the House Agriculture Committee and the numerous, separately organized commodity interests (for example, the National Cotton Council, American Wool Growers Association, American Cranberry Growers Association).[15] The concern of Chairman Cooley and the sugar interests was documented in Chapter 5. The implications for policy-making autonomy are obvious. When Presidents and their Secretaries of Agriculture have attempted to consolidate related programs, they have been met not only by the expected agency resistance but also by congressional veto. When the Kennedy administration proposed stricter production controls as part of the 1961 omnibus bill, the provision was deleted

---

[14] Ibid.

[15] Lowi, op. cit.; Douglass Cater, Power in Washington (New York: Random House, 1964) pp. 26–50.

by the agriculture committees in both chambers. No attempts were made to restore it during floor debate. In such an arrangement of tripartite reciprocal support, Presidential influence is at a minimum.

In these ways, constituency representation on committees and the congressional norm of specialization work to allow some large portion of agriculture policy to be decided by the interest concerned, with committees serving as one of the key decision-making units. Representation by commodity means further that the committee stage can be used for compromising among specific commodity interests. Thus a President's omnibus farm bill can be reworked at the committee stage to ensure satisfactory compromise among commodities represented on the committee.

However, the controversial issue of price supports and production controls which split the Congress and which split the committees could not be decided at the committee stage. Policy on price supports has been wrestled out in amendments and close votes on the floor. The change in the site of decision from subgovernment to floor may be tentatively explained by two factors. First, the committees themselves were split on the issue. Note the division in the House Agriculture Committee members in terms of commodities favoring high or low supports. Second, the political parties became involved in the issue and mobilized support pro and con to extend the conflict to wider congressional consideration.

THE PARTIES

The parties have taken clear and opposing stands on the issue of price supports and production controls, with the Democratic party supporting high price supports and strict controls and the Republican party opposing. In part, the party lines reflect distinct constituency interests. The high-support southerners and westerners have been predominantly Democratic. The corn-growing and dairy areas, which have opposed high supports, have been predominantly Republican. According to a 1962 study, specific crop interests with opposing views on price supports can be found underlying party interests. The party affiliation of congressmen representing districts ranking in the top twenty in the production of specific commodities was as follows:[16]

District's Commodity	Representatives	
	Democrats	*Republicans*
Rice	20	0
Peanuts	20	0
Cotton	20	1
Tobacco	17	3
Wheat	7	14
Dairy	4	16
Corn	2	18

Beyond constituency interest, however, the parties have served to organize congressmen indifferent to agriculture policy. Urban Democrats have voted with their more interested partisan colleagues for high price supports. Indifferent Republicans have voted against.[17] Through these alignments the parties have reflected basic ideological tenets as well as constituency interests: the Democratic party looking to the federal government for assistance to farmers, the Republican party being suspicious of "big government" and supporting the virtues of free enterprise and the laws of supply and demand.

The importance of party in congressional voting on price supports can be seen in the *Congressional Quarterly's* listing of key votes from 1947 through 1964. Of 34 key votes dealing specifically with price supports, all were party votes (where a majority of one party opposed a majority of the other party). On 22 of the 34 votes, an unusually high proportion, Republicans demonstrated strong cohesion, with 80 percent or more of partisan voting on the same side. Democrats exhibited 80 percent or stronger cohesion on 12 of the 34 roll calls.[18] Defection from party occurred when Republicans from wheat-growing constituencies voted with the Democrats for

[16] Editors of the *Yale Law Journal, op cit.* p. 76.

[17] See discussion in Chapter 3 as drawn from David Mayhew, *Party Loyalty Among Congressmen* (Cambridge: Harvard University Press, 1966), pp. 12–56.

[18] *Congress and the Nation: 1945–1964* (Washington, D.C.: Congressional Quarterly, Inc., 1965), pp. 677–679.

high supports, as documented by Mayhew. It occurred also when southern Democrats did not support a "northern" commodity price support and when specific geographical interests could be wooed to the nonsupport side. Thus in the 1949 fight over 90 percent parity versus a sliding scale of price supports, several western Senators switched to the sliding-scale side when sponsors agreed to include supports for pulled wool—a western crop.[19]

Price support legislation, then, was profoundly affected by party strength in Congress and the White House. Mayhew argues that House passage of high-support legislation required Democratic majorities of 230 or more. By the late 1950s, with increasing Republican opposition, passage required Democratic majorities of 260 or more.[20] And using *Congressional Quarterly*'s 34 key votes, it can be demonstrated that passage of high-support legislation was considerably more likely in a Democratic Senate or House and with a Democrat in the White House. Divided party control (that is Democratic Presidents with Republican congresses or Republican Presidents with Democratic congresses) brought divided results. Republican control brought passage of legislation favoring lower supports. Democratic control brought passage of legislation favoring high supports. (See Table 8.1.)

TABLE 8.1 Party and the Outcome of Price Support Legislation: 1947–1964[a]

	VOTE IN FAVOR OF		
PARTY CONTROL	HIGH SUPPORTS	LOWER SUPPORTS	TOTAL
Republican Congress-Republican President	0	3	3
Republican Congress-Democratic President	1	1	2
Democratic Congress-Republican President	9	6	15
Democratic Congress-Democratic President	12	2	14

[a] Based on the listing of key roll calls dealing with price supports, *Congress and the Nation* (Washington, D.C.: Congressional Quarterly, Inc., 1965), pp. 677–679.

[19] *Ibid.*, p. 677.
[20] Mayhew, *op. cit.*, p. 167.

The presence or absence of White House leadership may well have affected the amount of detection from one issue to another. On a number of the close votes recorded, such leverage may have made the difference. Presidents would seem to have affected agriculture policy outcome, but they did so through the stable alignments of party and constituency, as those latter were represented in the committees and membership of the Congress.

CONFLICT TO CONSENSUS: WATER POLLUTION

By the mid-1950s, Congress had ceased to debate whether there was a pollution problem and had turned to debate the federal government's role in pollution control. Pollution was not high priority for either the Eisenhower or Kennedy administration, and the fact that there was a debate and subsequent legislation at all was due in large part to the innovation and leadership of key congressmen. With legislative innovation and the conflict over federal role, much of the early policy-making on water pollution control can be told in terms of key committee members and the position and strength of the parties.

John Blatnik of Minnesota, conservationist and Chairman of the Subcommittee on Rivers and Harbors in the House Public Works Committee, and Senator Robert Kerr of Oklahoma and later Senator Edmund Muskie of Maine, chairman of the counterpart Senate subcommittee—these three men played a major role in committee initiation and floor management. Kerr was interested in the legislation, but opposed federal controls in the mid-1950s. He grudgingly yielded to Blatnick's efforts in the 1956 bill and gradually came to support some larger federal role by 1959. Blatnick led the successful effort for the 1956 Water Pollution Control Act, which included some controversial innovations of his own. The act authorized grants-in-aid to state and interestate agencies to assist in developing comprehensive water pollution control programs and matching grants to help localities construct sewage disposal plants. While Blatnik achieved most of what he wanted on the 1961 Act, he had to compromise to some extent with the Kerr forces.[21] After Kerr's death in 1963, Muskie led the Senate subcommittee with a fervor and initiative matching Blatnik's, resulting in a situation where both House and Senate subcommittees charged with handling water pollution legislation were headed by energetic activists. This may explain in large part why water pollution legislation in the 1950s and 1960s was very much a case of congressional initiative in legislation. Indeed, the one major delay in the 1965 bill—occurring at the conference stage to reconcile differences in the Muskie-Senate and Blatnik-House bill—appeared in some part due to the personal rivalry over *whose* innovative, strong antipollution legislation would go on the books. (Muskie's and the Johnson administration's did.)

With the issue raised of the federal government's role, the political parties were also of critical importance to the outcomes of legislation in the 1956–1961 period. In 1959, Blatnik attempted to amend the 1956 Act by increasing grants, setting higher limits on individual grants, and reorganizing the administration of the control program. Blatnik urged the creation of an Office of Water Pollution Control within HEW. At the time the program was bureaucratically buried in the Water Supply and Pollution Control Division, which was within the Bureau of State Services, which was within the Public Health Service within HEW. The Democratic congressional leadership supported the Blatnik bill, but the proposal countered the Republican view of a limited federal role and limited federal spending for what was considered state and local problems. The Public Works Committee and the House split on party lines in recommending the Blatnik bill. The House voted 240 to 156 for passage—Democrats voting 8 to 1 in favor, Republicans 10 to 1 against.[22] The Senate passed the bill 61 to 27, also on party lines. Democrats voted 48 to 8, Republicans, 13 to 19. Republican President Eisenhower vetoed the bill, with the famous message beginning, "Because water pollution is a uniquely local blight, primary responsibility for solving

21 Jennings, *op. cit.*, p. 101.
22 Sundquist, *op. cit.*, p. 330.

the problem lies not with the Federal Government but rather must be assumed and exercised, as it has been, by State and local governments." The Democrats fell 22 votes short of the two-thirds House majority necessary to override the veto. The House vote was 249 to 157, with only 27 Democrats and Republicans respectively defecting to the opposing party side.[23]

An analysis of House voting in support of water pollution control from 1956 through 1961 clearly summarizes the opposing position of the parties on the issue. (See Table 8.2.) It should be noted that through all these years, the Democrats had a majority in the House.

By the middle of the 1960s, the need for strict federal controls and federal spending was no longer in doubt. With growing public concern (and growing pollution), congressional conflict had changed to consensus. The 1965 Water Quality Act significantly strengthened federal antipollution laws and easily passed both Senate and House. After the Blatnik-Muskie compromise, the final vote was unanimous in both houses. By 1970, congressmen were rushing to get on the pollution issue. The Water Quality Improvement Act of 1970, the strongest pollution legislation yet written, passed the House, 392 to

TABLE 8.2 Percentage of Votes in Support of Water Pollution Control on Related Roll Calls in the House of Representatives, by Party: 1956–1961

		DEMO-CRATS	REPUB-LICANS	OUTCOME
1956	recommital	88	21	
1956	final passage	97	85	Act passed
1957	appropriations; deletion of funds	84	23	Deletion of funds was narrowly defeated
1959	recommital	89	9	
1959	final passage	89	19	
1960	veto override	90	10	No passage
1961	recommital	92	14	
1961	final passage	91	47	Act passed

SOURCE: M. Kent Jennings, "Legislative Politics and Water Pollution Control, 1956–1961," in Frederick N. Cleaveland, *Congress and Urban Problems: A Casebook on the Legislative Process,* (New York: Thomas Bavegy, 1969), p. 102.

[23] Jennings, *op. cit.,* pp. 104, 105.

1, and, the Senate, 86 to 0.[24] The weight of policy-making on pollution accordingly passed to the federal-state agencies charged with administration and control. but the congressional role had been critical in the earlier phases of innovation and mobilizing of support.

CONGRESSIONAL OVERSIGHT AND POLICY IMPLEMENTATION

Once a law is passed, congressional policy-making activity does not cease. In addition to legislating, Congress engages also in the activity of oversight: the supervision and, at times, influence over an executive agency's policy implementation. Oversight may involve as much policy-making as legislating. Its impact on policy depends on the focus and extent of congressional interest and the desire to influence administrative results. Some argue, indeed, that oversight is the most important function the contemporary Congress can perform. As initiative for legislation has passed to the executive branch, Congress finds itself less in position of lawmaker than in earlier American practice. But the need for some independent check of administration activity remains at least as critical if not more so than it was in the eighteenth century. Such supervision and control, in theory, can be ably performed by an independent branch organized into specialized committees and subcommittees, whose members are well placed to receive feedback on administration from constituents.

However, for some congressmen and committees oversight may involve merely the day-to-day interaction with administrative personnel in response to constituents' demands. Congressmen may "keep an eye on" what is going on in Immigration or the Forest Service and they may influence implementation on an individual ad hoc basis. But no formal or systematic attempt at supervision or control is undertaken. Of the more formal and systematic attempts, two different kinds of oversight deserve attention. The first is oversight by the substantive committee (over programs and agencies previously legislated on by the Congress). The second is the over-

24 Ibid.

sight that occurs through the appropriations process. The major site of policy-making at this stage, then—after proposal, hearings, passage, and administrative implementation—shifts back to the congressional committees.

COMMITTEE OVERSIGHT

Despite repeated urgings—from within Congress and without—for increased congressional oversight of administration by the committees, a number of factors limit that activity. The scale of priorities facing a congressman—or a committee—at any one time, the limited time of members already considered overburdened, the limited resources of committee staff and funds, all work against a vigorous employment of the oversight function. So does the need to maintain good relations with agency personnel in order to perform constituency service and not to "rock the boat" of a good working relationship. Oversight, then, incurs considerable costs in political resources that political men will not spend without a good return expected. According to Seymour Scher, "the typical pattern of committee review of the regulatory agencies is one of no review at all for long periods of time . . . interrupted by . . . a series of oversight bursts."[25] Under what conditions do these bursts of oversight occur?

Scher suggests five conditions under which benefits may well exceed costs.[26] One condition is partisanship. The majority party in Congress may attempt to embarrass the past or present opposition President who is held responsible for the agencies' appointees. Oversight appears to occur more frequently in situations of divided party control between President or Congress or frequent changes in the Presidential party. The new Republican Eighty-third Congress (1953–1954) initiated through its House Education and Labor Committee an intense review of National Labor Relations Board decisions. The NLRB was viewed as a Truman-appointed board, overly

[25] Seymour Sher, "Conditions for Legislative Control," *Journal of Politics* (1963): 540.

[26] The following discussion drawn on Sher's analysis, cited above, pp. 526–551. See also Sher, "Congressional Committee Members as Independent Agency Overseers," *American Political Science Review* (December 1960): 911–920.

friendly to labor. The committee gave three months of hearings to witnesses who claimed unfairness in the board's decisions and gave NLRB officials the last day to rebut the three months' testimony.[27] The Democrats returned the favor on the Eisenhower-appointed board by a subcommittee investigation in the Eighty-seventh Congress (1961–1962). Again in a divided-party pattern, congressional investigation of Sherman Adams and regulatory agency officials by the Legislative Oversight Subcommittee was carried out in 1958 under the auspices of a Democratic Congress.

The second condition is constituent or group interest. If committee members are dissatisfied with an agency's routine treatment of interests of importance to them, review may be initiated as a penalty or warning. The Democratic committee in the Eighty-seventh Congress under Chairman Adam Clayton Powell appointed Chicago Democrat Pucinski to direct a special subcommittee investigation of alleged racial prejudice in NLRB board's policy during the Eisenhower years. In the Eighty-third Congress, southern Democrats and Republicans on the House Education and Labor Committee felt the board was penalizing small employers at the expense of urban labor interests. These committee members from the rural South and small town and small city Republican areas had been opposed to union activity in large industry since the 1930s. They were even more opposed in the 1950s as organizing activity extended into the small industrialized areas of their own constituencies. With the urban Democratic members in opposition, the committee majority conducted hearings in 1953 directed at proposing "cures" for the NLRB from "an alleged lack of sympathy with the Taft-Hartley Act." The committee's orientation toward oversight rather than legislation in this case can be explained by two factors. The sharp division on the committee created legislative impasse. And no legislative initiative was expected from the White House for changes in Taft-Hartley. The relationship between routine interest representation and oversight should be noted also in its reverse form. Since agencies would prefer to avoid such investiga-

[27] Sher, "Congressional Committee Members . . . ," p. 915.

tion, routine decisions may be made wherever possible with an eye to committee satisfaction. The constituency service function, described in Chapter 3, is thereby supported by the *possibility* of oversight activity. It follows that members of committees where oversight is possible may have relatively better leverage over executive decisions regarding constituency interest than members on committees restricting oversight. The point will be elaborated later in the chapter.

The third condition, essentially based on constituency or group interest, is the committee's desire for agency protection against a threatened, more hostile investigation. Preemptive and protective in its aims, an investigation may be initiated to forestall inquiries from other, less sympathetic sources. The slogan used by committee and agency members is "better from your friends than your enemies." A variant on this practice is suggested by J. L. Freeman in his study of the politics of Indian affairs. When an investigating subcommittee of a hostile Senate committee brought out a damaging indictment of the Bureau of Indian Affairs, the commissioner persuaded the more sympathetic House committee to initiate its own investigation. The investigation was carried out and resulted in a report considerably at variance with the Senate's.[28]

The fourth condition is institutional loyalty: in particular, the perception by congressmen that the President is usurping traditional congressional prerogatives in regard to regulatory agencies, which, by the Congress, are considered "arms of Congress." It might be suspected that such institutional prerogatives vis-à-vis the Presidency become sharpest under the conditions of partisanship described above. The fifth condition is concern for new regulatory legislation. Inquiries may preface legislative consideration with the investigating committee wielding considerable influence over the forthcoming legislation by such an effort. The kind of hearings conducted, testimony received, and results reported may influence subsequent legislation.

---

[28] J. L. Freeman, *The Political Process: Executive Bureau Legislative Committee Relations* (2nd ed.; New York: Random House, 1965), p. 81.

Interests of the parties and of the committee members, then, appear to be major influences conditioning the extent of oversight activity. Yet given these influences, committees still vary in oversight. The variation in committees described in Chapter 5 may take us somewhat farther in understanding the conditions under which oversight may occur. John Bibby has examined the relationship between committee characteristics and oversight, with particular reference to the Senate Banking and Currency Committee.[29] Bibby documents the central importance of the chairman and, through the influence of the chairman, the importance of subcommittee structure and committee staff.

J. W. Fulbright, according to Bibby, was a "service chairman"—that is, "he permitted his Committee colleagues relatively free rein and would normally assist them where possible." With Fulbright's main interest in the Foreign Relations Committee rather than Banking and Currency, he leaned heavily on the subcommittee structure. Subcommittee chairmanships were assigned on the basis of interest and seniority, permitting committee Democrats with specific interests their own base of operations. A. W. Robertson was given the Banking Subcommittee, John Sparkman, the Housing Subcommittee, and Paul Douglas, the Production and Stabilization Subcommittee, where he could work for depressed area legislation. Fulbright allowed the subcommittees considerable autonomy, even to the extent of permitting subcommittee chairmen to pursue activities the chairman opposed. He maintained an adequate staff, urged them to keep up with administrative activities, and made available committee funds for hearings and travel.

With a service chairman, subcommittee autonomy, and staff support, Banking and Currency under Fulbright was modestly active in oversight. The Housing Subcommittee under Sparkman kept close watch on the policies of the HHFA (Housing Administration). The Small Business Subcommittee pursued the SBA (Small Business Administration). While Robertson as Banking Subcommittee Chair-

---

[29] John Bibby, "Committee Characteristics and Legislative Oversight of Administration," *Midwest Journal of Political Science*, (February 1966): 78–98.

man was not interested in investigating the Federal Reserve Board, some oversight of the board was carried on by the full committee. Fulbright began the practice of inviting the board's staff to the committee at the beginning of each new session to discuss its projected views on the economy. Under Fulbright's leadership, the committee undertook the Stock Market Study of 1955 to investigate agencies charged with regulation of stock exchanges. (Note its occurrence in a Democratic Congress with a Republican President.) Committee members felt that the board's change in policy following the hearings was a direct result of the critical investigation.

Robertson, Fulbright's successor as full committee chairman, is categorized by Bibby as a "restraining chairman." In the words of one staff assistant, "He's not an obstructionist so much as a drag. He won't obstruct, but he won't help."[30] Subcommittees were given less autonomy. The Banking Subcommittee, potentially a vigorous instrument for oversight of the Federal Reserve Board, was dissolved entirely and its business was handled by Robertson in the full committee. Clark's Subcommittee on International Finance was virtually moved out from under him. Fulbright wanted to take it with him to the Foreign Relations Committee and Chairman Robertson let it go. Proxmire, who wished to use his subcommittee to oversee the SBA, found himself with a minimum staff, which severely curtailed his plans for oversight. Committee funds became scarcer. The staff diminished in size with the result that few uncommitted resources of staff or funds were left available for oversight.

In addition to the chairman, subcommittee structure, and staff, Bibby lists two other factors affecting oversight. The two are interrelated: the members' interest in and orientation to the committee's work and the committee's recruitment patterns. Senate Banking and Currency is a relatively unattractive assignment. Assignments tend to go to members with low seniority and little experience in Congress. Further, member interest is low; most members who remain do so merely to keep the earned seniority. A similar complex was found for the House Foreign Affairs Committee, but not the Senate

<hr>

[30] *Ibid.*, p. 83.

committee. (See Chapter 5) Where interest in the subject matter does exist, according to Bibby, it is orientated mainly toward legislation and not oversight. With relatively junior members of low prestige in Congress and little interest in the committee's work, the number of members qualified and interested in effective oversight is limited.

Clearly, variation in committees affects the amount and kind. of oversight conducted. To investigate further, however, Bibby's inferences from the Banking and Currency Committee should be applied by students of Congress to a broad range of committee types and combinations of types as set forth in Chapter 5.

APPROPRIATIONS AND OVERSIGHT

An additional instrument of congressional oversight is provided by the appropriations subcommittees through their annual budgetary review of agency requests. Indeed, for some executive agencies, the oversight that occurs as a *by-product* of the appropriations process may be the only review they are subject to. Remarked one House Appropriations member: "You keep asking questions just to let them know someone is watching them." And a staff member remarked similarly: "You've got to shake 'em up once in a while. No one else will."[31] The House committee initiates the appropriations hearings and the legislation and carries the major congressional prestige in the appropriations process. The Senate committee acts primarily as a "board of appeals" for agencies after funds have been cut by the House. So it is the highly specialized House subcommittees that perform the bulk of whatever overseeing is done. Richard Fenno summarizes:

Committee members feel that a detailed and meticulous annual oversight of agency activity is essential, and they believe further that such an inquiry will yield examples of unnecessary expenditure. But even if no waste is found, they believe it is imperative that some legislative group

[31] Richard F. Fenno, Jr., *The Power of the Purse* (Boston: Little, Brown, 1966), p. 317.

with a concern for saving money keep the threat of inquiry hanging over the executive branch.[32]

It should be kept in mind, however, that oversight is incidental to the goal of the House committee—which is appropriating money for federal programs and in the process "guarding the Treasury" against executive waste, mismanagement, and overspending.

Human limits of time and energy make it impossible for the subcommittee to engage in any thorough review. Oversight is viewed essentially as an incremental operation. The subcommittee concentrates on what the agency has done in the past year and what it proposes to do in the coming year. In the words of one subcommittee chairman: "It's the changes we look at." The base of agency activity is left for the main part unexamined. Fenno's description is important:

The Committee does not, as a rule, probe deeply into well-established programs with well-established bases of support. What it normally does is to check carefully what the agency did with the increases it was given last year and inquire into the purposes for which the current increase is to be used. A program established last year or proposed for the coming year will receive careful scrutiny; and it is here that the program preferences of a key Committee member can work themselves most directly and decisively into legislative policy-making.[33]

Here again, decision-making differs according to the newness of the program. New programs receive the brunt of attention and attack. The more established a program is, the less it is subject to review.

Even with attention limited to program changes, a vast area remains for review. The subcommittee's needs for information can never be fully satisfied. Experience becomes a surrogate for information. Appropriations subcommittee members argue that experience gives a sense of where the problems are and where the waste may be. Indeed, repetition of the theme of "experience" in the interviews is noticeable. The following samples reveal how members view the problem of oversight and suggest also a rationale

[32] *Ibid.*, p. 316.
[33] *Ibid.*, p. 318.

for the norm of seniority as applied to the Appropriations Committee membership:

> After you sit on the Committee for fifteen years, you know these men and their programs, You become experts on them. . . .
> After you've been here and you've been through the budget before, you know the agencies and you know where to look. . . .
> Oh, you just feel it after a while and you've got lots of precedents to go by. . . .[34]

The committee's shared suspicion of executive spending programs facilitates operation of the oversight function. Unlike some substantive committees, there is no certain prior guarantee of sympathy between agency and subcommittee. Of course, degrees of sympathy and suspicion will vary. All agencies are not subjected to equally intensive scrutiny. Disregard of past committee directives may incur intensive questioning and threaten the entire program. Subcommittees develop confidence in some administrators and lack of confidence in others. One study of subcommittee oversight of four new agencies from 1949 through 1963 found that legislators spend more supervisory effort on agencies that spend the most money, whose requests have increased most rapidly, and whose behavior has deviated more frequently from subcommittee desires.[35] In addition, the policy interests of subcommittee members may motivate them to varying degrees of mildness or harshness in review. The Subcommittee on the Interior, it is interesting to note, has been deliberately weighed *against* westerners, in sharp contrast to the western dominance on the substantive Interior committees.[36] By contrast, the Subcommittee on Agriculture reflects the same farm constituency interests as the substantive committees. Fenno notes the subcommittee's admiration for the administration of three agriculture bureaus: the Soil Conservation Service, the Forest Service,

[34] Drawn from interviews conducted by Fenno, *The Power of the Purse*, p. 344.

[35] Ira Sharkansky, "An Appropriation Subcommittee and its Client Agencies: A Comparative Study of Supervision and Control," *American Political Science Review* (September 1965): 622–628.

[36] Fenno, *The Power of the Purse*, p. 365.

and the Extension Service. Administrators of the Forest Service were described by one subcommittee member as "dedicated men. They have the same kind of missionary spirit that a good minister has." Chairman Cannon of Appropriations, a one-time chairman of the Subcommittee on Agriculture, described the Extension Service as "the most popular of all federal farm activities."[37]

And yet with the overriding committee goal of allocating the federal finances with thrift and caution, the sympathetic relationships between Chairman Cannon and the Farm Extension Service appears to be the exception. Oversight can be a painful experience for administrations, as the following scene from a subcommittee hearing attests:

Subcommittee Chairman: I find a gentleman here, an FSO-6. He got an A in Chinese and you assigned him to London.
Agency Official: Yes, sir. That Officer will have opportunities in London— not as many as he would have in Hong Kong, for example—
Subcommittee Chairman: What will he do? Spend his time in Chinatown?
Agency Official: No, sir. There will be opportunities in dealing with officers in the British Foreign Office who are concerned with Far Eastern affairs. . . .
Subcommittee Chairman: So instead of speaking English to one another, they will sit in the London office and talk Chinese?
Agency Official: Yes, sir.
Subcommittee Chairman: Is that not fantastic?
Agency Official: No, sir. They are anxious to keep up their practice. . . .
Subcommittee Chairman: They go out to Chinese restaurants and have chop suey together?
Agency Official: Yes, sir.[38]

As that particular interchange makes vividly clear, the interests of both Appropriations Committee and executive participants are benefited by stabilizing the relationship between them—keeping uncertainty and conflict to as low a level as possible. For committee members, stability reduces uncertainty about administration and increases confidence in their own job performance. For the agency,

[37] *Ibid.*, pp. 379–381.
[38] Quoted by Aaron Wildavsky, *The Politics of the Budgetary Process* (Boston: Little, Brown, 1964), pp. 96–97.

stability helps program-planning and implementation and eliminates the fear of a subcommittee grilling where all sorts of embarrassing details may be revealed.[39] The attractiveness of an Appropriations Committee assignment and the resulting low turnover and high seniority of the membership work in favor of that stability. Bureaucratic routine does the same. Notice, however, the effects of a stabilizing relationship on oversight. As uncertainty is reduced, as agencies begin to *know* what the subcommittee will ask and will do, the power of potential oversight is also reduced. By contrast, new and controversial programs or agencies, especially those subject to partisan controversy, enjoy no such stability. In these cases the sweep and depth of the legislative oversight probe would appear that much more extensive.

The appropriations process, then, extends application of congressional oversight. It is limited to a review of incremental changes and to agencies that have not worked out a stable and sympathetic relationship with the relevant subcommittee, especially the subcommittee chairman. But it is supported in the oversight that it does undertake by the prestigious, experienced, cohesive, and highly motivated membership of the House Appropriations Committee. The committee seeks to guard itself against the "sympathy-leniency syndrome" it sees in many of the substantive committees. Skeptical of administration and with the power of the purse behind it, the House committee offers one continuing and highly effective mechanism for congressional supervision and influence over the executive.

SUMMARY

Policy-making takes place over time. As a program "moves" from innovation to continuing deliberation to implementation and oversight, the site of decision changes—from White House to floor, from committees to executive agencies, and back again. Yet at each site, the decisions made are very much a joint legislative and executive endeavor. Indeed, much of that interdependence derives from the

[39] Fenno, *The Power of the Purse,* p. 348.

knowledge that the site will change. It will change within one session. Presidential proposals are shaped by expectations of what the Congress will be willing to do. Committees report legislation knowing it will be defeated on the floor or in the other chamber. Agencies set appropriations requests, with an eye toward the relevant House Appropriations subcommittee, at a level high enough that the anticipated cuts will not damage the program and low enough not to arouse the subcommittee's suspicion or antagonism. And it will change from year to year. Presidential requests are geared to past years' defeats or victories; appropriations decisions to increments over past years' increases. It will change as congressional support becomes more firmly established or as President and congressional parties lose interest in an issue and relegate it to the concern of a subcommittee, agency, and clientele group.

With this view of a mutually dependent and reciprocally adjusting making of policy, the influence of congressional membership and organization can be more firmly appreciated. While new programs depend to some large extent on Presidential effort, their passage depends equally on the past recruitment patterns in the committee, the style and interest of the chairman, the strategy of the congressional leadership, and the number of partisans voting in support. The same holds for continuing programs, although in such cases the more established interest alignments in Congress may reduce Presidential leverage. The extent of a committee's oversight activity and the focus of the oversight—on program, agency, or issue —will be shaped in part by the strength of the interests represented on the committee and by the interest of the chairman or subcommittee chairman. It will be shaped additionally by the extent of partisan controversy and by the relationship between committee and party leaders. With this view also, congressional norms of specialization and seniority assume greater importance as principles by which Congress is strengthened in its influence vis-à-vis the executive. In his first visit to the Senate Foreign Relations Committee, Secretary of State Rusk was welcomed with the observation that he was the *seventh* Secretary of State one-third of the committee had had the pleasure of dealing with. Congressmen can claim a kind of experience that no President can match. "After you've been here fifteen years, you get to know. . . ."

One final point, implicit in the analysis above, deserves restatement. If Congress plays such an important part in policy-making and if the structuring and distribution of its membership help to determine the part it plays, congressional elections set in motion forces greater than most students of American politics (and voters as well) have recognized. Elections shape national policy by shaping the strength of party majorities, dictating committee majorities and chairmen, and influencing the selection of party leaders. And these are only the short-term effects. By returning incumbents, elections support seniority. They support stable patterns of interaction between committees and agencies and incremental policy-making. Party and committee leaders will return to their posts in following congresses. Policy will be made on the basis of what was legislated before. Elections shape not only the Congress of the present but its future organization and policy as well.

CHAPTER 9

SOME APPLICATIONS

*T*he study of political dynamics has concentrated on emerging rather than established institutions and has analyzed development and change rather than maintenance and reinforcement. Yet it seems clear that a dynamic is occurring as much in cases of stability as in cases of change. And until that process is understood, we know little about social and political life.

A study of Congress, then, may show in sharpest form the kinds of interaction and reinforcement involved in keeping things the way they are. This study has sought to isolate key points in congressional structure which, in interrelation with other points, form "complexes" of reinforcing action. Attention has centered on three points: the stability of membership, the structure of norms and values through which influence is distributed, and the leadership, with the primary explanatory emphasis given to the membership.

A number of specific interrelations can be identified. (1) The members' seniority explains emphasis on the norm of seniority and the seniority and stability of leaders selected. (2) The stability of leadership, in turn, reinforces the "value" of seniority and affects the practices of leaders. It enhances influence through recognition that the present leaders must be reckoned with for some time to come. It encourages cooperation between party and committee leaders and between the leaders of the two parties who must learn to live together for more than the span of one controversy or one

Congress. And it renders more understandable the nonideological character of much congressional action. Few issues are worth impairing the necessary long-term working relations. (3) The norm of seniority reinforces the stability of membership by making continued congressional service more attractive. (4) the stability of both members and leaders helps explain continuity in policy and reliance on incremental decision-making. Only new programs or major changes need intensive attention if the same membership has considered and voted for the older, basic programs before. (5) The structure of membership as shaped by electoral patterns and constituency interest affects committee and party cohesion. And this cohesion in turn may affect the committee's influence on the floor and clearly affects the success of the parties' legislative programs and the strategies selected by party leader and President. (6) Committee cohesion, attractiveness, and seniority appear to be interrelated, which increases the attractiveness of some committees and perpetuates committee characteristics and policy. (7) Committee assignments, as shaped by the leadership and members' self-selection, reinforce specific patterns of constituency representation and key institutional norms. If only "responsible legislators" are appointed to prestigious committees, the values of seniority, reciprocity, and compromise are given additional importance to members. If the "same-state" rule is applied to committee vacancies, it can be expected that the same-state interest on the committee will be perpetuated. (8) Norms of specialization and seniority reinforce each other. (Experience is said to increase knowledge.) And (9) both support constituency representation by the same interests on the same committees over a long period of time.

If all this sounds somewhat circular, it is. These separate interrelations form complexes of reciprocally reinforcing variables. Note the complex of support for seniority and for constituency representation by committees. And within the committee system, note the complex of factors perpetuating committee attractiveness and the kind of interests members represent. Clearly, there may be other such complexes—as yet unidentified. Once in operation, these factors reinforce each other. New members become part of an ongoing operation—in the Senate or House or in committee. They are influenced by its practices, and by their own interaction, they reinforce the operation of which they have become a part.

It should be clear that a study of this kind is limited by the literature on which it is based. A much more rigorous accounting is needed for many of the interrelations listed above, and they remain tentative until such an accounting is given. House-Senate and intercommittee comparisons are needed to test the effect of membership stability on norms and the separate effects of chairmen and membership recruitment on committee cohesion. Leadership skill, in both party and committee, needs to be isolated from the gross effects of partisan and factional numerical strength. Time-series studies are needed to trace the kind and rate of change in committee characteristics following a change in chairmen or membership.

Moreover, these interrelations require comparative testing outside the Congress. Are there, for example, common patterns of leadership selection that can be identified for collegially based groups? To what extent and on what dimensions will leaders embody key attributes of the members?[1] The present study found the predominant seniority of members capable of explaining the seniority of leaders and the stability of the leadership selection process. The likeness between members, party leaders, and committee leaders extended beyond seniority to regional attributes and electoral safeness. It might be worth investigating for other legislatures the frequency of mixed and matched patterns between senior and junior leaders and members. Identifying this and other similarities would

---

[1] For the importance of group structure as an influence on leadership, see Cecil A. Gibb, "Leadership: Psychological Aspects," in David L. Sills (ed.), *International Encyclopedia of the Social Sciences* (New York: Macmillan, 1968), Vol. IX, p. 99. For summary of related literature, see Gibb, "Leadership," in G. Lindzey and E. Aronson (eds.), *The Handbook of Social Psychology*, Vol. IV, (Reading, Mass.: Addison-Wesley, 1968), pp. 238–248. And note the conclusion of George C. Homans, *The Human Group* (New York: Harcourt Brace Jovanovich, 1950), p. 188: "The leader is the man who comes closest to realizing the norms the group values highest."

increase understanding of the particular institutional values stressed and give some broader understanding of the leadership selection process.

To what extent can recruitment practices explain the strength of norms and the particular norms that develop within institutions? Since norms are shared attitudes about proper behavior, it might be expected that they require a stable membership to develop. Do legislatures and such subinstitutional groupings as committees with relatively stable membership show a greater amount of shared attitudes on behavior than those subject to more rapid turnover? Congress with its clearly articulated structure of norms is a case in point. A study of the Connecticut state legislature indicates high turnover and low influence from the institution in developing shared attitudes.[2] One study of congressmen found increased similarity of role perceptions in nonfreshmen compared to freshmen, suggesting a homogenization of attitudes accompanying service in the Congress.[3] An additional instance is supplied at the committee level from the strong norms developed by the stable House Appropriations Committee. The question is complicated by the close relation in some legislative bodies between electoral competitiveness and turnover. Competition may dictate the degree to which members can afford to follow internal institutional norms as opposed to externally prescribed behavior—as from the constituency.[4] So one must ask if it is the competition or the turnover per se that is affecting norms. The question could be investigated with a sufficiently large number of cases and would seem well worth pursuing.

Recruitment practices may affect particular norms as well. Philip Selznick has suggested that leadership in hierarchical institutions may exercise a profound effect on institutional values by the recruitment policy that is employed. "Precarious values" may be buttressed,

[2] James David Barber, *The Lawmakers* (New Haven, Conn.: Yale University Press, 1965).

[3] Roger Davidson, *The Role of the Congressman* (New York: Pegasus, 1969), pp. 92, 93, 103.

[4] For research on a related point of competition and legislative roles, see John C. Wahlke *et al.*, *The Legislative System* (New York: John Wiley, 1962).

and changes in values brought about through the choice of new members.[5] While recruitment can be much less manipulated, it may be equally as effective in collegial groupings where the individual members have considerable importance: legislatures, committees, student bodies in universities, and departments of faculty. The available committee studies discussed in Chapter 5 suggest wide differences from committee to committee in recruitment of members —both from self-selection and the criteria applied by the party leadership—and wide differences in members' attitudes about the committee's work. What kinds of group attitudes are associated with different recruitment patterns? What are the correlates or the conditions under which recruitment affects attitudes? How does the role of the chairman or the existence of well-socialized senior members on the committee affect either the recruitment or the attitudes or both? More research on committees in Congress and elsewhere might well explore such questions.

Do the complexes of reinforcing factors observed in congressional action hold for other cases as well? Take the complex of committee cohesion, seniority, attractiveness of the assignment, and members' interest in the committee's work. Studies of nonpolitical groups have shown intercorrelations among these factors.[6] This could be tested for in other legislative committees and other political groups (and needs testing more extensively for the congressional committees as well). Given a politicized membership, divided at minimum on the lines of party and constituency, what are the conditions under which cohesion occurs? To what extent does the initial distribution of members affect cohesion and to what extent does group interaction or the leader's role alter the initial effects?

The first sounding of a subject necessarily raises more questions than it answers. But if this preliminary explanation of congressional

[5] Philip Selznick, *Leadership in Administration: A Sociological Interpretation*, (New York: Harper & Row, 1957), p. 57.

[6] See Barry Collins and Bertram Raven, review of "Group Structure" in G. Lindzey and E. Aronson (eds.), *The Handbook of Social Psychology*, Vol. IV, pp. 102 ff, 120.

stability makes sense, these are some of the questions which would be well worth pursuing.

THE CASE FOR CHANGE

Understanding the forces producing stability offers at the same time an understanding of possible change. It distinguishes changes that are likely from changes that are not. And it identifies key processes through which change can occur, for the same dynamic of interaction may be at work in either case. Reform the seniority system? But the seniority system is part of a reciprocally reinforcing complex of factors involving a stable, senior membership, deep-rooted institutional norms, and patterns of decentralized leadership. Overturn the present Speaker of the House? But Speakers are supported by the same complex of factors. Increase the vigor of committee oversight? But oversight is shaped by the prestige of the committee, the chairmen, and the partisanship and constituency interest of the committee members.

Distinguishing between fundamental institutional change and change in policy, this analysis suggests that no *internal* congressional factors may be looked to for institutional change, as inter-linked as they are with ongoing patterns of action. Leaders, for example, are products of the norms they uphold and perpetuate. With their position derived from institutional practices, they may be less than eager to use their position to change them. Moreover, leaders can go little farther than their committee and party majorities. But given the importance of congressional membership on internal action, the one point to initiate institutional change (as well as policy change) would appear to be in the selection of members. In other words, through congressional elections. It is difficult to imagine a House of Representatives, whose members averaged two to three terms' service, extolling the virtues of a seniority rule. Leaders might be selected for virtues other than experience and ability to compromise in a chamber that is young, subject to frequent overturn, and more strongly ideological. The foregoing analysis suggests that critical institutional change may come simply from the defeat of incumbents.

How easily can membership be changed through elections? Only recently has popular attention turned to congressional elections at all, and it may well be premature to say. However, the factors producing stability of membership—that is stable party loyalties and the tendency to reelect incumbents—accompany low levels of public interest and information in congressional affairs, as shown in Chapter 2. As the public becomes more aware that the parties and policy orientation of congressmen make a difference to national policy (and the 1970 elections may mark the beginning of such a trend), interest and information in congressional candidates should increase, with corresponding decreases in the stability of the membership.

For those concerned with policy change within the present institution, other points can be identified. Change can come after as well as through the elections, although elections would appear the stronger influence. Chapter 3 made clear the partial, unreliable character of much of the communication between congressmen and their constituencies, and the fact that on most issues the voting public is little concerned. Yet there is strong evidence to suggest that when a substantial portion of constituents (even a minority attentive portion) does care about an issue and communicates their concern, the congressman seeks to represent that interest in Congress. It can be argued that congressmen want to represent. They care about the mail. They count those for and against on specific issues. Change in specific policy, then, can come from a mobilizing of public support, with a longer-term change in orientation and patterns of representation on committees requiring a longer-term interest organization.

A third point of policy change is offered by the process of committee assignment. Committee assignments are only in part set by seniority and the policy of the leadership. Partly they are shaped by the desires of the congressmen themselves. If enough congressmen with a specific policy interest sought a specific assignment, change in committee membership and a corresponding change in committee action would occur. While seniority would restrain new members, a number of key decisions are taken by majority vote. A one-term change in the House Education and Labor Committee's membership brought the revolt against Graham Barden and the reporting of education bills. It is not a new idea. Southerners have been utilizing committee assignments for years to retain control of the Senate Judiciary and District of Columbia committees. But other congressmen with shared interests have not similarly exploited that potential. To take one clear example, the Senate Armed Services and Foreign Relations committees are both high prestige assignments won by Senators with some seniority but with very different liberal and conservative orientations and different views about war. What if antiwar Democratic senators with some political clout to start with began a concerted effort to win additional slots on Armed Services, rather than the more congenial Foreign Relations Committee? The party leadership would need to cooperate and the few doves who won their way through would feel isolated for a time. They would also be very junior. The idea would be difficult to carry out, but it suggests the kind of incremental, long-range strategy for change that could be seriously attempted.

A fourth point of change lies in the leadership. Leaders in the decentralized, collegial Congress may be less free than other leaders to initiate new directions in policy, but a potential is there which has rarely been exploited. Seniority guarantees independence from executive pressure. And within the constraints of collegialism and decentralization, congressional leaders are permitted a wide range of action. Consider the difference between Johnson and Mansfield in aggressive leadership; Dirksen and Knowland in Presidential support; the great differences in activity, extent of consultation with members, and leadership skill of the committee chairmen. Party leaders can effect change in the committee membership by a systematic selection over time, often invisible to all but the immediate interests concerned. Party and committee leaders can determine legislative outcomes by skill in scheduling or compromise and by the kind of leadership role they play.

An analysis of change needs also to specify the rate at which it may occur. Change may be dramatically sudden or imperceptible.

It may occur at swift or glacial rates. The record indicates that some short-term change is possible. Compare the Eighty-ninth Congress to its predecessor and successor, the Eighty-eighth and Ninetieth. The election of 47 new Democrats to the House, predominantly from the North, changed the committee ratios, changed the rules (specifically the 21-day Rule as discussed in Chapter 7), and brought new legislation to the books that had been sought in vain by Presidents for more than 15 years. In defeating large numbers of Republican incumbents, the election affected Republican seniority on committees and may well have contributed to Ford's defeat of Halleck as GOP minority leader. (See Chapter 6.) The Ninetieth Congress partially redressed the balance for the Republicans. The 21-day Rule was revoked and party ratios were again adjusted, but the aftermath of the 1964 Democratic landslide could still be felt. The Ninetieth Congress House Republicans were a junior group. Ford was still minority leader. Much of the Eighty-ninth legislation remained. Note also that these changes occurred through a turnover of only 47 out of a total of 435 House seats—or a marginal turnover of slightly more than 10 percent. Substantial change can come through marginal changes in membership at elections.

Other changes in policy orientation would take longer. Committees change their cast and their chairmen slowly. It takes slightly more than ten years on the average for a newly elected congressman to gain a chairmanship. (Democrats have taken 10 to 16 years, Republicans 6 to 12 years.) The point should be stressed to prevent would-be reformers from too early expectations and the resulting disillusionment. An institution persists and can be changed—only over time. Thus *groups that would produce policy change in Congress need some institutional persistence of their own.* Through the years, labor and farm groups have sought and won Congress to their way of thinking on major issues of concern. Peace groups could do the same. It seems not the "economic" nature of the interest, as some would say, that is the key to success, but rather organization, availability of grass-roots workers, and persistence—

persistence in mobilizing attentive publics and in talking with congressmen. Above all, it takes time.

Since discussions of change begin and end with the question of what should be changed, we can conclude by a broader assessment of what may and may not be expected of Congress in American political life. Despite much criticism to the contrary, it can be contended that congressional interaction with the public reveals, predominantly, a representativeness. There are key patterns of congressional action that work toward that result. The complex of factors relating to committee specialization encourages congressmen to become the experts and chief spokesmen on issues of primary concern to their constituents. Committee assignments facilitate corn districts' representation on the Agriculture Committee, water districts on Interior, labor districts on Education and Labor. The norm of reciprocity increases the influence of the interested member. Decentralized party leadership, which provides no means to force a member to hold to the party line, further encourages constituency representation. The voting behavior of congressmen shows that defection from party occurs mainly on those issues most salient to the constituency.

This representation is, of course, of a particular, partial kind. Congress represents the nation's geographical areas rather than a national public. It represents majorities—when they exist. The qualification is crucial. Given a sense of national emergency or need perceived by a *majority* of the public, Congress can act swiftly. The Emergency Banking Act of 1933, proposed in the first hours of the Roosevelt administration in a time of national economic crisis, was passed by Congress in one day. It streaked through both Senate and House, bypassing a number of usual stages in the legislative process. Indeed, the House debated and passed the "bill" without ever receiving a copy of it. There are, however, few issues in which a majority of the public is interested. Interest (and the lack of interest) is the key to congressional representation, as discussed in Chapter 3. Politics more typically involves a conflict of interested minorities, or a minority claim advanced with a majority uninterested and unaware. Where negative action is sought by a minority, the congressional committee structure is ideally suited for such a purpose. Thus retailers and chambers of commerce could convince Senate Banking and Currency Committee members not to support Senator Douglas' Truth-in-Lending bill. Positive action is difficult. Where positive action is needed, minority interests must survive the numerous obstacles built into the legislative process and compromise within the committee or the party structure. Within this organization, representation in Congress favors minority interests which are well organized and persistent. Given the "seniority" cluster of action, it also favors well-established over emergent interests.

As to its effectiveness as a governing agent, the preceding two chapters contend that it makes a difference to United States policy on a number of issues how many Democrats and Republicans are elected to the House and Senate, who the key committee and subcommittee chairmen are, what policy leaders have followed in past years in recruiting members to the key committees. Foreign aid policy changes with a change of a committee chairman. The Supreme Court has certain members rather than others because of the ratio of Democrats to Republicans in the Senate. The Senate and House do more than vote Presidential programs up or down; they shape White House expectations about what may be proposed—by the voting alignments of the members, the chairmen of the key committees, and the policy orientation of the committee members. Congress may cooperate or compromise with or oppose Presidents. But the point is that it *can* oppose. A major source of power lies in its potential for opposition—in its independence. This being the case, it is curious that the congressional practices most criticized are those that buttress this independence. The seniority system creates a committee leadership independent of party leaders including the President. Specialization in committees and subcommittees can generate subgovernments impenetrable to Presidential influence. Midterm elections counter the effect of Presidential coattails from the preceding election, cutting back after two years of a four-year term the first full strength of a President's partisan support. The impact of this independence on American national government should be clear. It means there exists an independent governing agent—which may on occasion be used as critic, check, or alternative route of representation vis-à-vis the Presidency.

More broadly, a particular kind of national policy is created through congressional action. It is a policy that is conservative, that is not innovative. New programs find the legislative process stacked against them. Majorities, in the public and in the public's representative assembly, are slow to form; but passage requires majorities in the committee and the floor, in the House and the Senate, all along the way. New programs and proposed increases in old programs receive the burden of attention from the Appropriations subcommittees in their annual review. The action that discourages the new protects the old. The incrementalism made necessary by the scope of responsibility and an overcrowded agenda means that established programs receive less review. With the stability of members, it can be expected that the same majorities which were created before can be mobilized again for their continuing support. Once formed, support consolidates, encouraged by seniority and specialization and the stability of leaders. The predominant congressional impact on government, then, is to discourage innovation and to produce continuity and predictability in public policy. (Predictability means that citizens in their dealings with public policy can count on the law not changing every two years or so.) This is a conservative effect, as the word is used to describe an attitude toward change. But the conservative impact is two-edged as regards the "liberalism" and "conservatism" of particular policies. It applies to innovation from the right as well as the left. Support consolidates for liberal as well as for conservative programs. The point is worth attention since "innovation" has strongly positive connotations in the current fashion. Congress, unfortunately for its popularity in the current fashion, is not predominantly innovative. From the individual citizen's standpoint, it will tend to discourage and dilute "good" and "bad," "necessary" and "dangerous" policy. It will obstruct liked as well as disliked Presidential programs.

The case for or against Congress, finally, comes down to the individual's ordering and balancing of political values: what he values most in kinds of representation, continuity and the capacity to innovate, and the power of legislative assemblies to check executives. When majorities want change, Congress can act with speed and effectiveness, but when minorities seek swift solutions to national problems, it may act slowly or not at all. It is sensitive to majorities, penetrable by persistent minorities, and much less sensitive to newly organized minority interests. It represents constituencies and a public that has been less than attentive to national affairs. This means that in times requiring high-mindedness and a national view, it may be transfixed by the parochial and the particular. Yet it has power to criticize and check the executive (who also may be transfixed by the parochial and the particular). Indeed Congress is probably the most powerful national assembly that can be found in political life.

This power—and persistence—are reasons enough to give it serious continuing study.